M000159915

The Standard & Poor's Guide for the New Investor

OTHER STANDARD & POOR'S PRESS BOOKS

THE STANDARD & POOR'S GUIDE
TO LONG-TERM INVESTING
by Joseph Tigue

THE STANDARD & POOR'S GUIDE
TO SAVING AND INVESTING FOR COLLEGE
by David J. Braverman

STANDARD & POOR'S PRESS

THE Standard
& Poor's
Guide for
the New
Investor

NILUS MATTIVE

McGRAW-HILL
New York | Chicago | San Francisco | Lisbon
London | Madrid | Mexico City | Milan | New Delhi
San Juan | Seoul | Singapore | Sydney | Toronto

The **McGraw·Hill** Companies

6 7 8 9 0   DOC/DOC   0 9 8

ISBN 0-07-141030-9

This publication is designed to provide accurate and authoritative information in regard to the subject matter covered. It is sold with the understanding that neither the author nor the publisher is engaged in rendering legal, accounting, or other professional service. If legal advice or other expert assistance is required, the services of a competent professional person should be sought.—*From a declaration of principles jointly adopted by a committee of the American Bar Association and a committee of publishers*

McGraw-Hill books are available at special discounts to use as premiums and sales promotions, or for use in corporate training programs. For more information, please write to the Director of Special Sales, Professional Publishing, McGraw-Hill, Two Penn Plaza, New York, NY 10121-2298. Or contact your local bookstore.

 This book is printed on recycled, acid-free paper containing a minimum of 50% recycled de-inked paper.

Library of Congress Cataloging-in-Publication Data

Mattive, Nilus.
  The Standard & Poor's guide for the new investor / by Nilus Mattive.
    p. cm.
  ISBN 0-07-141030-9 (pbk. : alk. paper)
  1. Investments. 2. Finance, Personal. I. Title: Standard & Poor's guide for the new investor. II. Title.
  HG4521.M359 2003
  332.63'2–dc21
                                        2003012941

Contents

Introduction

When I was young, the grown-ups around me were always complaining about money. Whether it was running off with Uncle Sam or just getting really tight, it seemed like money was never around when they needed it. Come to think of it, for never being around, money caused an awful lot of trouble in my house. Once, when my mom was especially distraught over her finances, I sheepishly walked over and declared that when I grew up, I would work in a money factory and make her all that she needed.

Of course, I now realize that I would never want to work for the Federal Reserve, and unfortunately, being a counterfeiter requires a much more sophisticated computer than the one I've currently got. However, I'm hoping that I can still print you the next best thing—some helpful advice on how to survive in a world ruled by money. While this book won't necessarily tell you how to *make* money, it will certainly tell you how to manage what you've got and how to ensure that you'll have even more in the future.

Although there are tons of books out there, I'm convinced that investors—young investors especially—are still in need of a simple, straightforward guide to personal finance from a source they can both trust and understand. Why? Because I have loads of friends with college degrees, great jobs, and not a dollar between them. I have other friends who earn the majority of their money through cash tips, which they spend as freely as the beer flowing on Saturday nights. I even know college kids who have taken out additional student loans to pay for plush city lofts. Very few of them understand what the S&P 500 is or how to open up a Roth IRA. And it's not their fault. My high school never offered a personal finance course, and I suspect most of theirs never did either. Moreover, our society is based on consumption, not preservation. So, in a time when the majority of Americans

[1]

have negative net worths, consider this book both a wake-up call and a road map for a better future.

While there are high school kids who trade stocks over PalmPilots, this book is not intended to teach you how to day-trade. Nor is it just for the trust fund set, even though they'd certainly be wise to take an active role in their financial lives. Rather, *The Standard and Poor's Guide to the New Investor* has been written for anyone interested in the basics of investing, from a salaried advertising exec to the lowliest lawn-mowing student. It will help you get on a sound financial path and explain the common types of investments, as well as how to evaluate them.

With knowledge, a little self-control, and a lot of patience, anyone can become a successful investor. The patience and self-control are up to you, but this book can at least give you the knowledge you'll need to begin. So, without further ado, let's get started.

PART 1

Personal Finance

CHAPTER 1

Getting Your Financial Life in Order

The best place to begin the path to successful investing is a lot closer to your wallet than it is to any fancy brokerage house. Why? There are two good reasons. First and foremost, without ever plunking down a dollar on an investment, it's likely that you can already make yourself richer. Second, examining the way your own financial life works can provide great insight into the way larger financial structures work. In this chapter, we're going to address a few universal concepts that will help you better manage your own finances.

Debt

Let's get started with two questions: Do you have any credit cards? If so, how much balance—or debt—are you carrying?

If you're an average American, you probably have thousands of dollars in credit card debt. Yes, that's right—according to Cardweb.com, an independent agency that monitors the credit card industry, in 2002 the average American household was carrying about $8400 in credit card debt. That number applies to households that have at least one credit card, or approximately 81 percent of all American households. Keep in mind, those outrageous balances were being charged an average interest rate of 14.71 percent!

Here are a few more credit card statistics (all from Cardweb.com):

1. **About 20 percent of issued credit cards have been "maxed out."** Credit card holders who have maxed out their cards currently owe interest on every dollar they were allowed to borrow. Of course, if this happens to you, odds are good that your credit card company will gladly raise your credit card's limit. Why? Because they want you to rack up an even higher balance. This ensures higher interest charges for them. Only when a credit card issuer thinks you've reached your debt threshold will they start reigning in your credit limits. Also, remember that the ultimate goal for credit card companies is to get you to pay the extremely low minimum monthly payment. That way they continue to earn interest on a larger sum of outstanding debt.

2. **The average credit card holder has eight credit cards.** While this statistic might seem unbelievable at first, it makes sense upon closer inspection. In addition to the big credit card companies, many department stores, gas stations, and other retail outlets offer their own private cards. Often, these private cards lure users through special discount programs. Even if the cards are rarely used, many people continue to carry them "just in case." As a side note, most credit cards remain active even after many years without use.

3. **At the end of the first quarter of 2001, total credit card debt in America stood at $660 billion.** The number is staggering, and even more so when you consider that one month of interest assessed at 14.7 percent gives us a collective monthly interest charge cost of over $97 billion.

Of course, averages are just averages. It may be hard to understand just how dangerous these debt loads can be. It may even be tempting to pay the minimum monthly amount every time the statement comes in the mail. But if you really want to make yourself richer, do not succumb to that temptation. Doing so will surely be detrimental to your financial well-being. What's worse is that it will negate any efforts you make in other investments. For a real world example, consider this:

Over the past year, Sally has accumulated about $1000 in credit card debt, at an annual interest rate of 15 percent (we're probably being overly conservative here). At the same time, she's been putting away $75 every month into an investment account that earns 6 percent a year. While contributing to an investment account is admirable, Sally would have done much better by paying off her credit card balance first, because dollar for dollar, she's losing 9 percent otherwise. To arrive at this conclusion, you need only subtract her winning investment—the retirement account—from her losing investment, the credit card debt. Yet even this is an oversimplified way of looking at it. If we assume that her credit card company applies the interest rate to her total outstanding balance, the amount she owes will spiral out of hand even more quickly if she either continues to let it remain or, worse yet, goes on charging away.

Check out Table 1-1. It illustrates just how powerful compounding debt can be.

This brings us to our first investing concept: **compounding interest**. The effect of compounding is like the power of a meandering river—slow to all appearances, but capable of changing entire landscapes over time.

In the case of accumulated debt, compounding can make breaking free a real task because as time goes on, the interest you owe gets tacked onto the initial amount you borrowed. So, you begin getting charged interest on the accrued interest as well as the **principle**—the amount you borrowed in the first place. At first this might not be a big deal. However, with time, it can accelerate the amount in question. The idea is to get compounding to work *for* you. More on that later. For now, let's focus on getting out of debt.

While the advantages of paying down unnecessary debts like credit card balances should be obvious, the truth is, many people fail to clean off their slates. Heck, there are people with $125,000 in credit card debt out there. Don't believe it? According to Myvesta.org, a credit counseling organization, the average debt involved in its most serious cases was $17,800 in 2000 and $48,200 in 2001!

TABLE 1-1. The Value of $1000 Initial Investment

End of Year	10% Interest	15% Interest	End of Year	10% Interest	15% Interest
1	$1,100	$1,150	19	$6,116	$14,232
2	1,210	1,323	20	6,728	16,367
3	1,331	1,521	21	7,400	18,822
4	1,464	1,749	22	8,140	21,645
5	1,611	2,011	23	8,954	24,891
6	1,772	2,313	24	9,850	28,625
7	1,949	2,660	25	10,835	32,919
8	2,144	3,059	26	11,918	37,857
9	2,358	3,518	27	13,110	43,535
10	2,594	4,046	28	14,421	50,066
11	2,853	4,652	29	15,863	57,575
12	3,138	5,350	30	17,449	66,212
13	3,452	6,153	31	19,194	76,144
14	3,798	7,076	32	21,114	87,565
15	4,177	8,137	33	23,225	100,700
16	4,595	9,358	34	25,548	115,805
17	5,054	10,761	35	28,102	133,176
18	5,560	12,375		Difference	= $105,079

However, this is not to say that all debt is bad. When used properly, even credit cards are a useful tool, for a number of reasons. They offer you a certain mobility that doesn't come with carrying around $5000 in cash. And many provide insurance on purchases too, which is extremely handy when the rental car agent is trying to convince you to take add-on insurance. Plus, some more competitive cards actually reward you for every dollar you charge, whether it's with cash rebates, discounts, or frequent flier miles. This puts an interesting spin on the matter, since someone in control of their finances can use their card for most of their purchases, pay off the balance every month, and actually get paid to do so. There's nothing quite like the feeling of getting an airline ticket at the expense of your creditor!

In additional, larger purchases, including cars and homes, often require loans, since most people don't have large sums of cash ready for deployment. However, what if they did? Would they be better off paying cash or borrowing? Although the answer depends on a number of factors, there can certainly be times when a loan would still make better sense.

For instance, let's say that John has inherited $42,000 and has decided to "invest" it in a sports car. (After a few more chapters, John may very well have better places to park his money.) Although he can easily pay cash, he has decided to investigate loans. His credit union is currently offering a 48-month loan at an annual percentage rate (APR) of 5 percent. At the same time, his bank has a money market savings account that is paying an annual interest rate of 4 percent. For simplicity's sake, we'll assume that the loan's interest is figured monthly and the savings account is figured at the end of every year. Also, John will be putting down $2000 on the car, making his loan worth $40,000. Table 1-2 shows what John will be paying in interest to the bank versus how much money he'll be earning on his investment.

TABLE 1-2. **Take a Loan or Pay Cash?**

Month	Monthly Payment	Remaining Amount	Monthly Principal	Monthly Interest	Cumulative Interest	Investment Balance
		$40,000				$40,000
1	921	39,245	754	166	166	
2	921	38,487	757	163	330	
3	921	37,727	760	160	490	
4	921	36,963	763	157	647	
5	921	36,195	767	154	801	
6	921	35,425	770	150	952	
7	921	34,651	773	147	1,100	
8	921	33,875	776	144	1,244	
9	921	33,095	780	141	1,385	
10	921	32,311	783	137	1,523	
11	921	31,525	786	134	1,658	
12	921	30,735	789	131	1,789	41,600

TABLE 1-2. (continued)

Mont'h	Monthly Payment	Remaining Amount	Monthly Principal	Monthly Interest	Cumulative Interest	Investment Balance
13	921	29,942	793	128	1,917	
14	921	29,146	796	124	2,042	
15	921	28,346	799	121	2,163	
16	921	27,543	803	118	2,281	
17	921	26,736	806	- 114	2,396	
18	921	25,927	809	111	2,508	
19	921	25,113	813	108	2,616	
20	921	24,297	816	104	2,720	
21	921	23,477	819	101	2,822	
22	921	22,654	823	97	2,919	
23	921	21,827	826	94	3,014	
24	921	20,997	830	90	3,105	43,264
25	921	20,163	833	87	3,192	
26	921	19,326	837	84	3,276	
27	921	18,485	840	80	3,357	
28	921	17,641	844	77	3,434	
29	921	16,793	847	73	3,507	
30	921	15,942	851	69	3,577	
31	921	15,087	854	66	3,644	
32	921	14,229	858	62	3,707	
33	921	13,367	861	59	3,766	
34	921	12,502	865	55	3,822	
35	921	11,633	869	52	3,874	
36	921	10,760	872	48	3,922	44,995
37	921	9,884	876	44	3,967	
38	921	9,004	879	41	4,008	
39	921	8,120	883	37	4,046	
40	921	7,233	887	33	4,079	
41	921	6,342	891	30	4,110	
42	921	5,447	894	26	4,136	
43	921	4,548	898	22	4,159	
44	921	3,646	902	18	4,178	
45	921	2,740	905	15	4,193	
46	921	1,830	909	11	4,204	
47	921	917	913	7	4,212	
48	921	0	917	3	4,216	46,794
					4,216	6,794

As you can see, John would actually be better off taking the loan and investing the lump sum over the four years. This assumes that he will then use other income to pay off his car over the four years (which is advisable anyway). Also, we didn't include the effect of taxes. Still, the result certainly runs contrary to common sense. Very few people would borrow at a higher rate than their rate of return on an equally sized investment (and in most cases, they'd be smart not to). However, two factors make this particular case work. First, the terms of the loan are a big contributor. Since an annual percentage rate only applies to the remaining amount owed on the loan, John is actually going to pay about 10.5 percent of $40,000 in interest over the four years. Meanwhile, compound interest is boosting his lump sum's rate of return over the same time, to the tune of about 17 percent. A few lessons can be learned from our example:

1. It's worth repeating—the effect of compounding is a force to be reckoned with.

2. Often, figuring out the true value of an investment takes some, well, figuring.

3. Everything has an **opportunity cost**. What's that last one, you ask? Simply put, opportunity cost is the difference between two potential options. It can usually be broken up into dollars, although things like time can also be considerations. In the above example, the opportunity cost was the difference in the money earned.

Another advantage that often arises from taking on some debt is better **liquidity.** In the above example, it's the ability to get at the cash in a money market rather than having the money tied up in a car. That way, in the case of an emergency, the money would be readily at hand. The idea of liquidity is another important concept to keep in mind, and we'll talk more about it in just a bit.

Taxes are often an additional factor in the great "carrying debt" debate. This is especially true in the case of buying a home, where the interest on the loan is tax deductible. Without getting into the messy details, suffice it to say that you will generally be able to subtract the amount of interest you pay on a home loan from the amount of income you get taxed on. While tax breaks shouldn't be the primary reason for buying a home, they can certainly make taking out a large loan a bit more manageable.

At any rate, debt is generally a barrier to financial success because it automatically handicaps your ability to earn money from other investments. This is because the rate of interest you owe on borrowed money will have to be subtracted from the rate of interest you earn on another equal investment. And despite our example above, a general rule of thumb is: "If you have cash, use that . . . unless you can find an investment that will earn more interest than the rate you're borrowing at." Simple enough, right?

So, if you don't have any debt, good for you. If you do, let's talk about how you can get out of it. One particular word comes to mind: discipline. Actually, even if you don't have any debt, discipline will still be one of your greatest allies in the world of investing.

This is mainly because discipline will enable you to formulate a plan and stick to it. (And any good investor has a plan.) When times get tough, or jeans go on sale, discipline will be there to keep you on the straight and narrow.

In the case of credit card debt, you have a few options. If your balance is not that large, or you happen to have enough in savings to cover the amount you owe, you are best served by paying it off immediately. As we've already seen, it's almost certain that you're not earning nearly enough money anywhere else to compensate for the rates your credit card company is charging you. If you are, please disregard the rest of this book and begin penning your own. If you can't pay off your debt in one lump sum, you'll need to develop a plan of action, which will be based largely on what you earn and what you can afford to allocate toward the debt.

Since most short-term debt is owed to credit card companies, here are a few steps you should take right off the bat:

1. *Stop charging.* While it's going to be difficult, the best way to get out of debt is to stop accumulating it. According to one source,

the average American has six and a half credit cards. Of course, the average American would be better off if all credit cards were halved. When you're out of debt and capable of better managing your money, you might consider getting one card that rewards you for purchases, but only if you're confident that you can stay on top of your balance. If you lack the faith, keep tossing out those applications you're constantly getting in the mail.

2. *Consolidate your debt.* This step is about assessing how much interest each of your balances is being charged. When comparing the rates, be sure you're comparing apples to apples—look closely at the rates and factor in hidden fees. Speaking of fees, it may also be possible to negotiate with your credit card company—just as they'll often waive late fees, they may also lower your interest rate rather than have you take your debt elsewhere.

3. *Start paying off the debt you have.* Begin allocating a set amount to your credit card balances, preferably as much as you can. While it's best to pay off the highest debt first, some people may feel more comfortable tackling the smallest one, since they will see the most progress there. No matter which way you decide to go, the key is getting into a rigid routine. Which brings us to the next topic.

Budgeting

In a nutshell, budgeting is about managing the money coming in (**income**) and the money going out (**expenditures**). In the business world, this is known as **cash flow**. What you're shooting for here is positive cash flow. In other words, more money coming in than going out. But if you're not there yet, don't feel bad—neither are a lot of companies.

We will begin by assuming you have some sort of income. If so, it's likely that you already have the potential to be much richer than you think. A good way to prove this to yourself is by keeping track of your expenditures for a month or two. You might think of this as your own personal **statement of cash flows**. Please note—writing down only major purchases won't do. The key here is following every dollar that comes into your hand and every dollar that goes out.

Carry around a pad of paper and write down how much you spend, when you spend it, and, most important, what you spend it on. If you use an ATM, keep track of how often you visit it in a month and be sure to include the fees you're assessed for its use. If you're like most people, what you find will be startling—$20 on 20 cans of soda (when three dollars for three two-liter bottles yields the same amount), 50 bucks for that doohickey (now collecting dust) that you bought from the television shopping channel, and 300 smackers for that handbag— but it was marked down from $700! You get the idea. Yet this is not to create a world of penny-pinchers, it's simply to give you an idea of where your money is going. From there, you can make your own assessment of how wisely those dollars are being spent.

Time for an example. We'll do a before and after:

Bob is a clerk earning $400 a week (after taxes). Every morning on the way to work, he stops at his favorite coffee house, Fourbucks Coffee, where he spends, you guessed it, four bucks on coffee. He goes there even though he can get free, albeit subpar, coffee at work. Heck, paying four bucks doesn't seem that outrageous while he's sipping his caffeine-laced latte. After all, it gets him up for work, doesn't it? Still, Bob makes a note of the expenditure every morning.

At the end of the month the tally is in: Bob spends about $80 a month on coffee alone (he makes his own coffee on the weekends). Keep in mind, $80 is 5 percent of Bob's monthly take-home pay. By simply drinking the coffee at his office three times a week, Bob reckons he can save himself $48 a month. Heck, if he bites the bullet and foregoes the designer coffee completely and instead deposits the money in a savings account, he'll have $960 at the end of the year! Ten Fourbucks-free years from now, by depositing that amount every year in an account earning 4 percent interest, his savings would be worth $13,407.93!

A little more analysis shows that Bob stops at the ATM a few times a week, where he pays $1.50 for every withdrawal. Not only do these frequent stops add up to wasted dollars, they also give Bob way too many chances to make impulsive withdrawals. Instead, he would be much better off by constructing a budget. A quick glance at his regular monthly expenditures looks like this:

$400 a month for rent

$250 a month for food

$80 a month for coffee

$40 a month for gym membership

$50 a month for bills

$150 a month for car payment

Total = $970 a month

Bob generally blows the rest of his money on miscellaneous items— movies, video games, CDs, etc. In fact, before he kept track of his expenditures, he would have been hard pressed to tell you where the money went at all.

Saving

Clearly, Bob can organize his finances a little bit better. For instance, he may decide that every month he absolutely needs to spend $890 on the basics (rent, food, car, gym, bills). On a weekly basis, that amounts to $222.50. To be fair, he gives himself an extra $50 a week for anything else he wants or needs. The other $127.50 a week will go into a savings account—unless there are outstanding debts that need to be paid off first.

Bob's best bet is to find out if his company offers direct deposit. If they do, he should automatically have this amount deposited into a savings account. If not, he'd be wise to march that check right down to his bank and immediately deposit the fixed amount. The rest can go into his checking account, from which he'll withdraw $220 every week (leaving a little money for the ATM fees every time).

The key here is discipline: Barring any major catastrophe, Bob is never to withdraw from his savings account. However, he also never needs to feel obligated to carry over any money from his weekly $220 either. This is the beauty of a budget—once it's implemented, you can just sit back and let it work to your advantage. No more post-purchase cognitive dissonance (ahem, buyer's remorse). No more wondering whether you can afford something either. Most of the time, getting started is the hardest part.

Bob's life may not be completely analogous to yours. Still, chances are good that you have some money dripping away somewhere. With some careful analysis and a little discipline, you should be able to plug some leaks and get well on your way to a more secure future.

What all of this boils down to is living below your means. Have you ever noticed that a lot of people seem like they're always just squeaking by? Better yet, how many times have you heard someone say, "I really can't afford it, but I just had to have it." In the end, it's that sort of thinking that leads to a heaping pile of problems. While we all love the romanticism of *buy now pay later*, the truth is, most of us will live far too long to ever benefit from such notions. As a new investor, your first job may very well be to replace fanciful thinking with the boring-but-profitable truths of life.

At this point, you're probably thinking that none of this sounds like much fun. In fact, it may very well sound like *work*. While it is in fact work, you will eventually realize that it's rewarding work. At first, missing your daily designer coffee may sting. You may even go into some convulsive fits. However, at the end of the month you'll feel good about not getting a whopping credit card bill. And after a few more months, you'll feel even better when your bank statement shows a big, fat positive number. It's really a trade-off—a few little snips here and there will ultimately give you a more stable financial platform, and hopefully a much better night's sleep. Unless of course you're one of those people who's okay with $125,000 in credit card debts. If so, get thyself to a rather good bankruptcy lawyer immediately.

Why Invest Anyway?

So far we've been talking a lot about paying down debt, controlling expenditures, and, most important, getting into a regular routine of saving. The next logical question is: Where do you start putting that money? This will be our first foray into the real world of investing.

Perhaps the first place you were ever taught to put your money was in a piggy bank. That might be thought of as a low-yield investment. **Yield**, in the broadest sense, is the payoff you can expect to get from a particular investment. The word also has a similar, but more specific meaning when it comes to stocks, but we'll talk about that later. Getting back to that piggy. The reason why a piggy bank is a good learning tool but not a good investment is because the money you put in just stays put; it never gets any fatter. In fact, in an inflationary environment, it's actually shrinking as time goes by.

In a what, you ask? **Inflation** occurs when the cost of goods and services rise. No matter how old you are, you've probably heard stories about something "that used to cost a nickel." Whether it be a taxi ride or a phone call, the real prices of things have risen throughout time. So, in order to keep up, investors attempt to increase their own money at a faster rate. In a sense, that's what getting richer really means—the ability to buy more than you once were able to. That makes the rate of inflation the number one thing investors are trying to beat. Although deflation—a time when the cost of goods and services declines—is also a possibility, that's not something investors focus much attention on. For an illustration of what sort of inflation the American economy experienced in the 20th century, check out Table 1-3.

As you can see, things got quite a bit more expensive over that period. Heck, James Dean paid $7000 for his brand new Porsche 550 Spyder back in 1955. Buying a brand-new Porsche now would cost anywhere from 6 to 20 times that amount. And inflation can work a lot quicker than you think—a dollar locked away in a piggy bank during 1980 would have only been able to buy about 50 cents worth of stuff in 2001. The lesson here is: If you plan on investing your money for a high-powered sports car, you should either start paying for acting lessons or put your savings somewhere other than a piggy bank.

But where?

There are a number of assets you can invest in. **Physical assets** are tangible things like houses or Porsches. Other popular physical assets include "collectibles," like coins, jewelry, works of art, and so on. Some physical assets, like houses, suit both living needs and investment needs, since historically, housing prices have risen over time. In addition, physical assets often provide a certain level of emotional comfort to their owners. It's reassuring to be able to *have* something to show for your money. In the case of a painting, it may be enjoyable to look at as well.

Another category of assets is **financial assets**. This category covers a number of less tangible items, including stocks, bonds, CDs, money markets, and traditional bank accounts. While financial assets represent much more than just pieces of paper, they are an indirect and less tangible form of wealth. In fact, many people often perceive financial assets as the great unknown, gaping black holes that money goes into but from which it never returns. The truth is just the opposite. Although your money won't be parked in your driveway, financial assets will often generate cash returns through dividend or

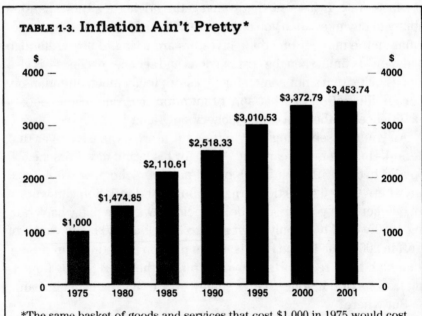

TABLE 1-3. **Inflation Ain't Pretty***

*The same basket of goods and services that cost $1,000 in 1975 would cost $3,453.74 in 2001, for an increase of 245%. (Based on the consumer price index.)

interest payments. And like the best physical assets, the face value of many financial assets will also increase over time.

Earlier, we mentioned the idea of liquidity—how readily an asset can be turned into cash, or how easily something can be bought or sold at a fair price. Liquidity plays a large role in how attractive a particular asset is.

Consider physical assets for a moment. Over the past 10 or 20 years, real estate prices have gained considerably. However, there can be a significant drawback—a lack of liquidity. While most financial assets can be bought and sold relatively quickly, a house may take a significant amount of time to sell. This is because financial assets are bought and sold almost every day and the marketplace for them is national, if not international. In addition, most financial assets are easily appraised—one share of a particular company's common stock is identical to every other. Often, in a single day, such shares have hundreds or thousands of buyers and sellers who establish, through their transactions, the asset's current value. Conversely, a house is generally a unique asset—many a buyer has walked away because of a particular house's layout. In other words, the uniqueness can often make matching up a buyer and a seller much more difficult. A particular asset's liquidity should always be a consideration as you investigate its individual merits and inherent risks.

With any asset, there is risk. However, the kinds of risk vary from investment to investment. As we just noted, liquidity can be one example of a risk. Inflation, which we've already covered, is another risk. But there are a number of additional risks.

Since economies are cyclical, there is always **economic risk**: the chance that economic conditions will turn sour for a certain investment. Sometimes, the economy can become bad for almost all investors. The depression of the 1930s is a good example. A related risk is **interest rate risk**—the risk that interest rates will become unfavorable. For example, rising interest rates are generally bad news for bond investors.

Speaking of bond investors, **credit risk** is the possibility that a company may not make timely payments on its outstanding debt. In the worst cases, the company never pays back what it owes. While credit risk is especially relevant to bond investors, it also impacts stockholders. And mutual fund investors must always contend with **manager risk**, the chance that the person running the fund will make bad decisions, ultimately costing investors money. If that's not enough, foreign investors, or domestic investors holding foreign investments, face **currency risk**—the possibility that currency exchange rates will negatively impact their holdings. Lastly, there is just plain old **market risk**, which affects just about any investor. Sometimes, whole markets crash, as the American stock market did in both 1929 and 1987. During one single day in October 1987, the entire stock market lost more than 20 percent of its value, wiping out gains that had been made over two years. Many investors lost large portions of their portfolios, and shifted their remaining money into safer assets.

Okay, enough risk. Let's continue talking about reward. Really, you should approach any investment by gauging its risks versus its rewards. While you may never be able to fully assess them, you can usually get a good idea. There's pretty much a direct relationship between the two—the more risk you take on, the greater your pay-off should be if it works out. For example, a very risky stock may quadruple your money if the company succeeds; however, if it fails, you might lose all of your initial investment. For a better idea of the risk-reward relationship, see Table 1-4.

As you can see, stocks in all of their various forms are riskier than other assets. This is because they have been subject to far greater swings in value over short periods. However, as you will see later, they have also provided the greatest historical returns. Bonds, another risky category, have also proven profitable over time. However, neither stocks nor bonds are good places to park money that you may need at a moment's notice.

So before we get into the real heavy hitters, we should first look at the more common vehicles for savings. It's also worth noting that even sophisticated investors generally maintain at least one or two of these as short-term savings accounts, since they're far more liquid than other investments. Examples are basic savings accounts and money markets. Certificates of deposit, which are less liquid, are also popular choices.

TABLE 1-4. The Risk-Reward Tradeoff

The return from various investment choices tends to vary according to the risk.

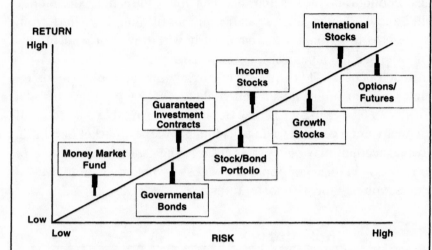

Note: The depiction above is intended to indicate general, long-term levels of relative risk and return.

A basic **savings account** is the typical bank account. It is sometimes referred to as a passbook account, since many banks provide account holders with little books used for keeping track of activity. The main advantage of a basic savings account is its accessibility—the money is pretty much there whenever you need it, and you're free to add or subtract at will. They can also be opened with relatively little money. And the Federal Deposit Insurance Corporation (FDIC), a governmental agency, usually insures these accounts for up to $100,000, providing one last level of security. Of course, the disadvantage is that these accounts typically provide a comparably low rate of return.

A **money market** account can be thought of as a restricted savings account since you're only allowed so many withdrawals per month. In addition, they tend to require a higher balance than basic savings accounts—to open one may take as much as $2500. However, you will be rewarded with a higher interest rate.

Lastly, there are **certificates of deposit**, or CDs, which usually provide investors with more favorable interest rates than most savings accounts and money markets. The downside is that your money will be locked away for a specific amount of time, anywhere from six months to a number of years. Early withdrawal of your money will often lead to a penalty.

Which is best? This will be a recurring theme. It all depends on what your particular needs and goals are. If you plan on buying a house in a few years, a CD may be the safe, profitable way to go. If you just want a general savings account, a money market or a basic savings account may be a better choice. The easiest way to think of all of this is in terms of opportunity cost—what you gain in ease of access, you pay for with lost interest.

Summary

The first investment you make is in yourself, by paying down your debt, and starting to regularly save money. The best way to accomplish all this is through a budget. Keep track of where your money is going and look for places where you can trim back. Give yourself a monthly amount of money to spend and start directing a separate amount toward existing debt or into an investment . If you need a short-term place to put this savings, you may consider a basic savings account, a money market account, or a certificate of deposit. While any of these will reward you with some form of interest, the amount will vary depending on how freely you can withdraw your money.

CHAPTER 2

First Investing Steps

You now know the merits of paying off debt first, establishing a budget, and setting aside some short-term savings. And you realize that investors are, first and foremost, battling inflation. Now it's time to explore some more basic investing concepts.

Setting Goals

Just as in managing your personal finances, the best place to start is with a plan. With your budget established, you should have a reasonable idea of how much you can afford to invest on a regular basis. The next step is figuring out what you're investing for.

As we said, money designated for short-term events is best kept in safer havens like savings accounts. And although others may tell you differently, the short term is anything less than five years. Why not buy the next hot stock and double your money in a year? Because even if you knew what the next hot stock was, **volatility**—the tendency of an investment to fluctuate—would be working against you. In other words, when it comes time to buy that house, your stock may be in the midst of a slump (even if it ultimately doubles, triples, or quadruples).

While there's just no telling how well a volatile investment will be performing at a given time, the longer your time horizon, the better off you are. This is because the risk of loss tends to diminish with time. For historical proof, look at Table 2-1.

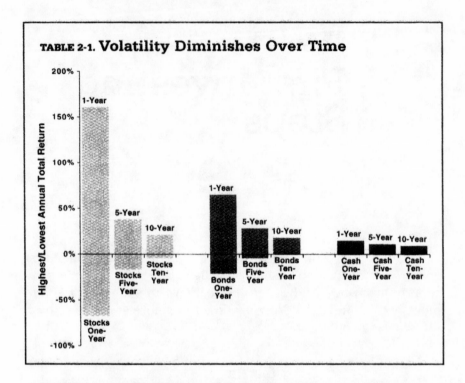

TABLE 2-1. Volatility Diminishes Over Time

Generally, a major long-term goal is having enough money for retirement. Later, in Chapter 12, we'll discuss the various retirement accounts commonly available. For now, it's enough to boil it down to one simple concept: If your company sponsors a matched retirement plan, your first long-term investing dollars are usually best put there. These types of programs reward you for investing in your retirement by literally matching the contributions you make. Usually, they also lower your taxes.

Your company will specify what percentage of your contributions it will match, and often the rates will change along with the amount you put in. In addition, there are ceilings on how much money you can contribute to these plans, which also limits how much your company can ultimately give you. Sound confusing? It's really not as bad as it seems. While the specifics of this type of account will be covered later, here's an example of how it works.

Hector makes $40,000 a year and his company currently offers a matched retirement program. For the first 3 percent of his salary that Hector contributes, his company will match 100 percent. For the next 3 percent, the company matches 50 percent. Anything Hector contributes beyond that goes unmatched. If his budget allows, Hector would be wise to contribute at least 6 percent to his retirement account since every dollar will benefit from some sort of matching. By contributing $2400 (6 percent of his $40,000 salary), Hector automatically earns a rate of return of 75 percent, or $1800. He is unlikely to find a guaranteed rate of 75 percent anywhere else on the planet.

Of course, no matter what type of account you use for retirement, you'll need to figure out the particular investments you want your money to go into. In addition to the basic investments already discussed, the next few chapters will teach you more about other common options, including stocks, bonds, and different types of funds. Again, a lot of the choices you make will depend on what stage of life you're in, what your goals are, and how comfortable you are with risk. However, some generalizations can be made, and they may help you find a place to start.

One common piece of advice in this area is: "The younger you are, the more aggressive you can be." As previously discussed, the longer your time frame, the less likely you are to be harmed by volatility and the more likely you are to be helped by things like compounding interest. While this is not a certainty, historically, time has been on the side of patient investors. In addition, younger people can usually look forward to a growing stream of income, which further mitigates the inherent risk of more aggressive investing. A corollary to this rule might be: "Start early." All other things aside, simply starting to invest early can make a major difference in how much money someone makes from an investment.

Let's take, for example, two different people, Sara and Amador, each of whom earn a 10 percent compound return on their money over a 40-year period. Sara puts in $2000 a year for the first eight years, representing a total investment of $16,000, then stops. At the end of the 40 years, her $16,000 investment will have grown to be worth $515,188. Meanwhile, Amador waits until the eighth year before he begins investing anything. However, for the next 32 years (years 9 through 40), he puts away $2000 a year. All told, Amador has invested $64,000—four times as much as Sara. Yet, at the end of the 40 years, his investment will only be worth $378,496, or 75 percent of Sara's.

Table 2-2, below, illustrates just how powerful starting early can be.

TABLE 2-2. The Power of Starting Early

Year	Early Funding Contribution	Year-End Value	Late Funding Contribution	Year-End Value
1	$2,000	$2,200	$0	$0
2	2,000	4,620	0	0
3	2,000	7,282	0	0
4	2,000	10,210	0	0
5	2,000	13,431	0	0
6	2,000	16,974	0	0
7	2,000	20,871	0	0
8	2,000	25,158	0	0
9	0	27,674	2,000	2,200
10	0	30,441	2,000	4,620
11	0	33,485	2,000	7,282
12	0	36,834	2,000	10,210
13	0	40,517	2,000	13,431
14	0	44,569	2,000	16,974
15	0	49,026	2,000	20,871
16	0	53,929	2,000	25,158
17	0	59,322	2,000	29,874
18	0	65,254	2,000	35,061
19	0	71,779	2,000	40,767
20	0	78,957	2,000	47,044
21	0	86,853	2,000	53,948

TABLE 2-2. (continued)

Year	Early Funding Contribution	Year-End Value	Late Funding Contribution	Year-end Value
22	0	95,583	2,000	61,643
23	0	105,092	2,000	69,897
24	0	115,601	2,000	79,087
25	0	127,161	2,000	89,196
26	0	139,877	2,000	100,316
27	0	153,865	2,000	112,548
28	0	169,252	2,000	126,003
29	0	186,177	2,000	140,803
30	0	204,795	2,000	157,083
31	0	225,275	2,000	174,991
32	0	247,803	2,000	194,690
33	0	272,583	2,000	216,359
34	0	299,841	2,000	240,195
35	0	329,825	2,000	266,415
36	0	362,808	2,000	295,257
37	0	399,089	2,000	326,983
38	0	438,998	2,000	361,881
39	0	482,898	2,000	400,269
40	0	531,188	2,000	442,496

Diversification

But time is only one factor in smoothing over the volatile nature of investments. No matter when you start, the idea of **diversification** will be crucial for your success.

Simply put, diversification is spreading your money throughout a number of investments, in order to reduce risk. Diversification will help your **portfolio**—your collective investments—stay on a smooth path upward.

There are at least two different levels of diversification. The first is **asset allocation**: investing in more than one type of investment, such as stocks, bonds, and cash. The second is diversification within asset classes. With stocks, this might mean buying a number of different companies that do different types of things. For bonds, it might mean buying a few different types, with varying maturity dates.

Asset allocations, like all aspects of your portfolio, will change depending on a number of factors, including age, goals, and risk tolerance. As we already discussed, generally, the younger you are, the more aggressive you can be. In the case of asset allocation, this means your portfolio can be more heavily weighted toward stocks, which have historically grown at a faster rate than other investments. Check out Table 2-3, below—it shows some model allocations for different times of your life:

TABLE 2-3. Sample Allocations for Different Investment Time Horizons

Kind of Investment	40 Yrs.	30 Yrs.	20 Yrs.	10 Yrs.
Large-cap U.S. Stocks	50%	50%	50%	45%
Mid-cap U.S. Stocks	15	10	10	5
Small-cap U.S. Stocks	10	10	5	5
International Stocks	25	20	15	10
Bonds	0	10	20	25
Cash Equivalents (Money Market, CDs, etc.)	0	0	0	10
Total	100%	100%	100%	100%

The asset allocation of your portfolio often plays a bigger role than the particular investments you purchase within a given category. It may actually be the most important long-run determinant of the return on an investment. This is because different assets perform well under different economic conditions.

Consider this: As the phases of the economic cycle come and go, you want to be in a position to benefit. But since it's difficult to anticipate when to shift into and out of currently favorable assets, the diversified approach—where funds are continuously committed to a variety of asset classes—will generally work best. Many investors try to time cycles, even day-to-day price movements, and although you may hear otherwise, very few are successful at it. This is not to say that you shouldn't pay attention to economic and market conditions; however, if you have a long-term time horizon, you will be best off with a consistent, diversified approach to investing.

Beyond the basic difficulty in predicting the future, there's another reason why constantly shifting your investments diminishes your returns: **frictional costs**. These are the costs you incur by enacting transactions. Essentially, they consist of the fees you pay for buying and selling investments as well as the taxes you'll likely owe on any money made.

Of course, over the long term, shifting your asset allocation from time to time will make sense. This is less because of economic conditions than due to changes in your needs and goals. Again, young—and single—investors can afford to be more aggressive because they have more time to ride out a downturn in the market. But parents or grandparents may not be able to bear the same level of risk.

Of course, no generalization can totally do an individual situation justice. While a younger investor is usually advised to allocate a large percentage toward stocks, a goal like the purchase of a home may actually make the investor better off in a more conservative investment. Meanwhile, someone nearing retirement, who would typically be advised to allocate a large amount toward fixed-income investments like bonds, may be better off keeping it in faster-growing stocks if the money is destined for a grandchild.

An easy way to set and keep track of your asset allocation is to use a rebalanced method of weighting. Simply put, this technique consists of setting a fixed percentage of your portfolio to a given asset class. As the percentages change, you simply reallocate funds to bring the preplanned percentages back into line. For example:

Linda is fairly young and has decided that she will be investing for her retirement 30 years from now. She's been putting 70 percent of her money into stocks, 20 percent into bonds, and the remaining 10 percent into cash equivalents (a money market, in this case). Recently, stocks have been performing pretty well. Because of this, they now comprise 80 percent of her portfolio. To rebalance her portfolio, Linda must sell some of her stock holdings and put the proceeds back into the bond or cash sections of her portfolio.

To some extent, using this method forces you to sell high and buy low—the basic, but elusive, goal of all investors. In Linda's case, she was forced to take some profits from her stock investments. And as the old Wall Street adage reminds us: "No one goes broke by taking profits." The rebalancing method is effective because it keeps a set amount of money in each investment, allowing profits from currently favorable investments to be put to work in the investments that are likely to outperform next (keep those cycles in mind). While there's no rigid rule about how frequently you should rebalance, once a year should suffice for most investors.

Once you have your asset allocation worked out, you'll have to figure out how you'd like to distribute your investment dollars within each allocation. The next few chapters will give you a lot more information about this, but a general foundation can be laid out now.

Within stocks, you'll want to spread your money out between a number of different companies. Something like 20 stocks scattered across different industries may do the trick. With bonds, you may opt for a number of different types, with varying maturity dates and risk levels. In either case, you may also choose to use funds instead (more on this in Chapter 10).

However, you also need to be careful that you don't overdiversify by having too many investments. Doing so will only make managing your investments more difficult, and may even hinder the results you desire. Often, investors with complicated portfolios fail to realize that many of their investments mirror their other investments. Take someone with a number of mutual funds in their portfolio. Many times, some of their funds are holding the same stocks; thus, the perceived diversification is nothing more than added complexity.

In short, maintaining an appropriate asset allocation, as well as diversification within asset classes, will help smooth out the performance of your investments over time. While it will limit the overall performance of your portfolio to some degree, the risk protection it provides makes it more than worth it. And as we've already discussed, time works in tandem with diversification to help mitigate risk.

Let's go back to those investors who lost out in the crash of 1987 for a minute. We previously noted that many who were affected by the market's sudden collapse ended up shifting their remaining stock holdings into safer investments. In retrospect, that wasn't such a great move. By shifting their assets into safer havens, those shell-shocked stock investors missed out on the tremendous gains that followed the crash of '87. For example, $10,000 left in the stock market after that decline would have been worth about $23,000 by the end of 1993. In comparison, the same $10,000 in a safer investment, such as a money market, would have only grown to roughly $14,000. This is a prime example of poor asset allocation, since it goes against the basic premise of letting each category work its magic over time.

Of course, just as it's not wise to invest all of your money in one particular investment, it may also be unwise to invest it all at one time. Because economies and markets are cyclical, you wouldn't want to get caught putting all of your money into investments at the wrong moment. By investing over time, you add yet another layer of diversification to your portfolio.

One strategy employed by investors is called **dollar cost averaging**. Simply put, it means regularly putting a fixed amount of money into a given investment. For example, someone holding a stock might purchase $100 of the stock every month. In doing so, the investor's **cost basis**—the average price paid for an investment—stays at an advantageous rate (assuming the stock appreciates over the longer term). How? Because if the stock goes down, the investor's $100 purchases more shares than it could have if the stock had gone up. And if the stock goes up, then the investor buys fewer shares at the higher price, but makes gains on the shares already held.

Note that this strategy is vastly different than, say, purchasing a fixed *number* of shares on a regular basis. Table 2-4 illustrates the difference.

TABLE 2-4. An **Example of Dollar Cost Averaging**

Here are two ways of investing $50,000:

Year	Price Per Share	Choice A		Choice B	
		Shares Purchased	Dollars Spent	Shares Purchased	Dollars Spent
1	$50.00	200	$10,000	200	$10,000
2	25.00	200	5,000	400	10,000
3	37.50	200	7,500	267	10,000
4	62.50	200	12,500	160	10,000
5	75.00	200	15,000	133	10,000
Total		1000	$50,000	1160	$50,000

Although dollar cost averaging is best applied to big name stocks, it can also work with other types of investment. And it works especially well for people with steady incomes, since they can afford to set and maintain a preplanned schedule. It's also a perfect strategy for retirement plans, since most people regularly contribute to them and they tend to have a long time-horizon.

Taxes and Investing

Taxes are yet another concern for investors, and any good strategy takes into consideration how taxes may affect an investment's results. Because every investor's tax situation is unique, and because the laws themselves change so frequently, it's difficult to cover the subject at length. Still, a few general concepts can be explained here.

The good news is that most capital gains are taxed at favorable rates. Based on changes in the tax laws in 2003, capital gains made on investments held longer than 12 months are taxed at 15 percent, which is much lower than the average income tax rate. The reason behind the lower rates? To encourage investment. Any profits made on investments held less than a year, however, get taxed as regular income.

Through retirement accounts, many investors are also able to defer taxes, or pay them later rather than sooner. This is yet another reason why contributing to a retirement plan is a smart way to start your investing path. We'll talk more about the tax advantages of various retirement accounts in a later chapter. As you'll also see in a later chapter, many bonds offer certain tax advantages too.

It's important to figure taxes into your calculations when comparing your investment choices. The difference they can make is startling. In fact, the tax advantage afforded to long-term capital gains is another big reason why long-term investing approaches work so well. And this only becomes truer as your income level increases. To get an equivalent **net profit**—the amount you actually take home—a short-term investor in a higher tax bracket would have to make a far greater initial percentage gain than someone just letting time and a more favorable rate work their magic. Want proof? Consider the two styles of investment in this example:

John and Frank both fall into the 35 percent tax bracket, meaning their regular income is taxed at 35 percent. Under the capital gains laws, any long-term capital gains they make will be taxed at 15 percent. Both are excellent stock pickers. However, Frank is an impatient sort. While John buys $10,000 worth of stock and holds onto it, Frank furiously moves his $10,000 from stock to stock (see Table 2-5). After a year, John sells his investments, which have doubled to $20,000. All told, he owes $1500 to Uncle Sam. Meanwhile, Frank has made 150 percent on his initial $10,000, for a grand total of $25,000. But because he bought and sold his stock a number of times within the year, his $15,000 gain is taxed at 35 percent. This means he pays $5250 to the tax man. So, before we even consider the fees for all of Frank's transactions, John has already won, even though his investments earned much less than Frank's. What's more, John also took on less risk in the process!

TABLE 2-5.

Start	John $10,000	Frank $10,000
December	Buys $1,000 worth of ten different stocks	Buys $10,000 worth of stock
January	Holds position	Sells stock at a 20% profit
February	Holds position	Buys $12,000 worth of stock
March	Holds position	Holds position
April	Holds position	Sells stock at a 25% profit
May	Holds position	Buys $15,000 worth of stock
June	Holds position	Holds position
July	Holds position	Sells stock at a 60% profit
August	Holds position	Holds cash
September	Holds position	Buys $24,000 worth of stock
October	Holds position	Holds position
November	Holds position	Sells stock at 4% profit
December	Sells all stock for a total of $20,000	Holds $25,000 in cash
Profit	$10,000	$15,000
Profit %	100%	150%
Tax Rate	Long-term Capital Gains flat rate (15%)	Short-term Capital Gains profits taxed as regular income (35%)
Tax Owed	$1,500	$5,250

This is a prime example of why trying to trade your way to a brighter future probably won't succeed. Of course, more than a few investment professionals might encourage you to do just that. This is mainly because the other half of those frictional costs—the commissions—might go to them. The practice of frequently changing a portfolio is commonly known as **churning**. And although some frequent traders are very successful, your best bet is to stay away from a professional who encourages this sort of behavior. Chances are good that they don't have your best interests in mind.

This raises a good question: Should you seek professional help in making investment decisions? We'll help you answer that in the next chapter.

One last thing to note is that research will play a large part in your path to successful investing. Of course, the research needn't be limited to poring over volumes of financial statements or worrying about the recent movement of bond prices. The financial markets are inherently tied to current events around the world, so most of the things you read on a daily basis can help shape your investment decisions. You're researching just by reading the newspaper every morning.

Many investors—among them, Peter Lynch, as will be discussed later—have endorsed the investment philosophy of "buying what you know." In other words, your own experiences, both professionally and as a consumer, can provide valuable insight into potential investment trends. In the chapters ahead, we'll talk more about how to go about the specifics of researching each particular type of asset. For now, recognize that investments are real things in the world, not just abstract figures.

Summary

The best way to start investing is with one or more goals in mind. Once you have your goals established, you'll be able to develop a plan to get you there. Of course, any good investing plan will involve making sure that you're not too exposed to any one particular type of investment. And for most goals, a longer-term approach is better. Also, don't forget that commissions and taxes can detract from your progress, so always try to keep your transactions to a minimum.

CHAPTER 3

Getting Professional Investing Help

There are a number of different ways to go about investing, especially when the question of professional help arises. One main factor in deciding what approach is best for you is how much time and effort you want to spend along the way.

Along with money, time is something every successful investor needs to put into a portfolio. Just researching potential investments can take hours on end. In addition, overseeing your current investments can be an exhausting, and stressful, experience. However, for investors who are willing to take matters into their own hands, it's more than possible to build and maintain a solid portfolio without much outside help. In many ways, the Internet has made it easier than ever before. Willing investors can now research and manage their portfolios completely online. However, other people may feel more comfortable getting outside help. Some may even prefer to leave most of the decision-making to a professional.

So, what kind of professional services are out there?

Stockbrokers and Other Brokers

The first and perhaps the most common investment professional is the stockbroker. Although we'll be devoting a whole section to the world of stocks later in the book, it makes sense to talk about stockbrokers now.

[37]

Essentially, a stockbroker is a sales representative for a larger organization, known as a brokerage house. The level of service you'll get from a stockbroker varies according to the individual you choose and the philosophy of the larger organization. Brokers, who are licensed to buy and sell investments for their clients, act as intermediaries for investors.

While stockbrokers are widely talked about, there are other types of brokers as well, such as bond brokers. For our purposes, most of what we say about stockbrokers will also apply to other types of securities brokers. And while there are different types of brokerage houses, which we will discuss in depth later, you'll most likely encounter individual stockbrokers at full-service brokerages, or those that provide their clients with more than just basic trading services.

The first thing you'll need to know about a potential broker is whether his approach matches your investment style. If the guy you're thinking about going with talks a mile a minute about the "next great thing" when you've already told him that you want to buy stable investments for the long term, then you should probably look elsewhere. In fact, if something about someone just doesn't sit well with you, you're better off considering other candidates. After all, this is an important relationship. You'll be entrusting your money to this person, and you'll need to know that they have your best interests at heart. You'll also want to know that they're reliable.

Also, double-check how your broker gets paid. As we've already said, most brokers make their money by charging a fee for every order they place for you. The problem is, this doesn't necessarily align their interests with yours. While the commission route isn't necessarily bad, more than one less reputable broker has been known to constantly trade in and out of investments in an effort to increase the commissions paid by a client. If you're uncomfortable with this possibility, there's another way to go. Some brokers, especially those who operate as financial advisers, take a percentage of assets under management, which is a fancy way of saying "your money." This system actually encourages your broker to help you make sound decisions, since what's yours is his.

Financial Advisers and Planners

The financial adviser category of investment professional is a tricky one, primarily because it's a catchall for investment professionals. In fact, whenever stockbrokers seem to be getting a bad rap from the investment community, a whole new crop of "investment advisors" suddenly appears to take their place. While anyone who helps you make investment decisions is, in the broadest sense of the phrase, an adviser, a true financial adviser will help you look at the larger picture, such as the overall construction of your portfolio, rather than just what stock to buy next. As we said, investment advisers are also more likely to charge you based on the money they're helping you manage, instead of the many investments you buy or sell.

Financial planners take things even one step further, since they often also deal with tax considerations and estate planning. In fact, true financial planners will have taken a series of courses designed to teach them the ropes. Those who have, and who have passed a test on the materials, are given the title of "certified financial planner," or CFP for short. In fact, some CFPs may not be directly responsible for purchasing your investments for you. If you decide to consult a certified financial planner, find out exactly what services they're offering and just what type of transactions they can handle for you.

Checking Out an Investment Professional

No matter which type of investment professional you decide to go with, you'll want to do some investigating first. Some good things to look at are:

1. **Credentials**. There are many different licenses and certifications that an investment professional can have. For example, the Series 7 is required of investment professionals involved in marketing

stocks. And beside the CFP designation, there are others, like the CFA, which stands for "chartered financial analyst."

2. **Experience**. There may be nothing more valuable to an investor than finding someone who has been involved in the investing world for a long time. Investment trends and fads come and go; someone who's been around long enough should be able to steer you away from learning lessons the hard way.

3. **Recommendations**. Someone may look very good on paper, with a great background and years of experience. But there's nothing more telling than talking to a few of their clients. Any reputable adviser should be happy to provide you with a few references. While they'll surely give you the names of happy customers, you may still be able to learn more about their approach and whether it suits your preferences. Just make sure you aren't talking to his mother or someone who happened to get a lucky pick. The best people to talk to are longtime clients, who've been through good and bad times. They'll have the best insight into what your broker's style is really like. In addition, you may be able to ask the initial references if they know any other clients you can talk to. Since many clients come to a broker through word of mouth, you might be able to use this in reverse to your own advantage—often, talking to someone who's no longer a broker's client will help balance the glowing references you're likely to get from current clients.

4. **Legal check**. Finding out if your potential investment adviser has ever had legal complaints from previous clients should be relatively easy. First, you might want to ask the candidate directly. Also, you might do a little digging of your own. The Securities and Exchange Commission (SEC) and the National Association of Securities Dealers (NASD) should be able to tell you if brokers have ever had complaints filed against them. While one or two disgruntled investors might not necessarily indicate a bad candidate, a number of complaints is certainly a warning flag.

Other Professional Advice

Having an investment professional is only one approach to getting outside help. If you're simply looking for some advice but prefer to make your own decisions, there are a number of other sources to consider. Many investors subscribe to services that give them investment recommendations, market forecasts, or other useful pieces of information. Some common examples include *The Wall Street Journal, Investor's Business Daily*, or Standard & Poor's *The Outlook*. A number of popular investment publications are listed in the appendix.

Also, as we noted before, the Internet offers investors a wealth of information. There are thousands of websites with everything from real-time stock quotes to the latest market headlines. In addition, online communities allow investors to get together for informal chats on their favorite companies, economic conditions, and virtually every other topic they can think of. For a list of some popular web destinations, see the appendix.

Concerning online information, however, it's important to realize that many other web users will also be novice investors or, worse, they might be sophisticated investors who are trying to profit by spreading false information (for more on investment scams, see Chapter 13). Never act upon something you discover online unless you've validated it through your own research.

Clubs and Other Organizations

One last way to get outside investment advice is through an investment organization. There are many large groups out there. One of the largest, the American Association of Individual Investors, is comprised of many smaller, local chapters. In addition, the AAII frequently features guest speakers, many of whom are experts in their fields.

Other investors choose to form their own investment clubs. These can range from informal meetings among friends to more serious gatherings where everyone in the group is required to do their fair share of outside investment research before each meeting. Joining one of these clubs is a great way to share your investing experiences with other like-minded people.

Summary

Getting professional investment help is not for every investor. However, if you'd feel more comfortable having someone lead the way, be sure to check them out thoroughly. Also, even if you don't want someone to take care of your transactions for you, it would probably be a good idea to consult a few sources of investment information from time to time. Even most professional investors spend countless hours reading newspaper articles and business publications as well as visiting websites.

PART 2

Stocks

CHAPTER 4

What Are Stocks?

Stocks. The name conjures up Wall Street, big money investors, maybe even that guy at the party who always has some hot tip for you. But what are stocks really? The short answer is that stocks represent a partial ownership in a given company. Some companies don't really offer stock; others only offer it to certain people behind closed doors. Those companies are considered "privately held." However, many other companies, including a lot of the well-known brands in this country, are "public companies," or "publicly traded." What this means is that these companies, in an effort to raise money for their current and future operations, have decided to let anyone purchase a stake in their business. That's why one unit of stock is known as a **share**.

Often, a core group of people will retain a majority of the stock in a given company. This is especially true in cases where founding partners or families are involved. By having a large chunk of stock, these people are able to exhibit a certain level of control over what direction the company heads in. In the end, a company may choose to offer only a small percentage of ownership to outside investors.

There are different types of stock, including **common stock** and **preferred stock**. Common stock is what most investors purchase—it gives the holder basic ownership of the company and a vote equivalent to the number of shares held. The key here is "ownership" —that's why stocks are considered equity investments—because as an owner of part of the company, you benefit when the company benefits and lose when the company loses.

[45]

This is different from an investment in a bond, because as a bond-holder, you are only a lender. You expect to get back your initial investment plus the specified interest, but that's it. While the repayment is tied to the business's success (a failed business can't pay you back), you only get back what you agreed upon. Essentially, the upside of a bond is limited. If you're a part owner in a business, in contrast, you can theoretically reap infinite rewards if the business continues to grow and prosper.

Preferred shares entitle their holders to certain extra rights, including the right to get paid before other shareholders should the business fail (though bondholders still come first). Let's back it up and look at how a business might evolve in the real world:

Dale has been shaping surfboards in his garage for a few years and has gotten pretty good at it. He's made some for his friends and they've all been satisfied with his work. Word is starting to get out, and as a result, a number of people have been asking Dale if he'll make them boards too. He figures that the money he'll get from the orders is enough to warrant shaping surfboards full-time.

Of course, he can't keep operating out of his garage; he'll need to find a space to run his business. The problem is, renting a space and getting all of the materials he'll need to build the boards is going to cost money, and his customers aren't willing to pay in advance. So Dale turns to his savings. He figures he has enough to buy the materials he'll need to build the boards, but he'll have to look elsewhere for the money to rent a shop. He asks around, but no one is interested in loaning him the money, especially not the banks. After all, if the business fails, they'll lose their investment, and if the business succeeds, all they'll get is the same interest they could get from other, safer forms of lending.

Dale realizes that he'll have to do more to entice people to give him the start-up money, and so he offers a wealthy friend a stake in the business in exchange for some money. The wealthy friend, who has used one of Dale's boards, recognizes the potential that the business holds. Believing that a little money now might turn into a whole lot more later, she agrees to put in the money.

A lot of businesses actually start out this way, and the individuals who contribute funds are called **angel investors**. Often, they won't even be friends with the entrepreneur; they may simply believe in the person's work. Based on the promise of the business, they'll lend start-up money, which is also known as **seed capital**. Usually, an agreement will be drawn up between the angel investor and the entrepreneur outlining the relationship, and that'll be it. In Dale's case, he decides to give his angel investor 10 percent of the business in exchange for some start-up money. A few months go by and the business has been doing well. Dale has a nice little shop and enough orders to last him a year, but somewhere in the back of his mind he begins to worry. What if someone sues him? What about the taxes on his business? What if his shop burns down? After consulting with a lawyer, he decides that the best way to protect his business is to incorporate it. In other words, Dale's business will become a separate entity in the eyes of the law. It will be based in a certain state and be subject to certain rules and regulations. At the same time, Dale will be one step removed from the potential dangers of operating a business. If a board breaks and someone is injured, the corporation, not Dale, will be sued. And if business turns bad, Dale's personal finances will remain somewhat separate from those of the corporation.

Of course, lawyers cost money. Plus, Dale now realizes that he'll need better tools and more materials to keep growing the business. He's even been thinking about hiring a couple of people to help him do some of the work, and that will take even more money.

The angel investor suggests that they look into getting some **venture capitalists** to invest in the business. These are investors who specialize in funding early-stage companies. Many times, venture capitalists will invest in certain industries where they can offer expertise in addition to money. In exchange for these things, they look to receive a portion of the business.

This stake comes in the form of a **private placement:** a block of stock that is given directly to investors. In this case, Dale finds a venture capital firm that specializes in sporting goods. He presents his business plan to them, and they decide to give him additional funding in exchange for 15 percent of his business. They also put him in touch with a marketing firm and a cheaper foam supplier. Dale has completed his first round of venture capital financing.

With this additional money, Dale rents a much larger shop and hires ten workers. He even begins letting a few of them shape surfboards so he can meet the steadily increasing demand for his boards, which are now being sold in a number of shops up and down the coast. Meanwhile, the marketing company that Dale has been consulting with has done a study. They've found that Dale's name is getting so popular that many surfers have expressed interest in buying hats, T-shirts, and swim trunks with his company's logo on them.

Since he doesn't have the experience or the resources to produce these other products, Dale realizes that he'll need more money, so he turns to those venture capitalists again. This is what's known as a second round of venture capital financing. The venture capitalists like the prospects of this new business and decide to give him more money. With it, he hires a few people to design and manage his clothing line, which will be produced by an outside company.

A year or two more go by, and Dale's business has hit it big. Kids all across the country are wearing his clothes, even if they don't surf at all. The venture capitalists, who now have a reasonable stake in Dale's business, think it's about time they cash out. After all, venture capitalists usually invest in early-stage businesses and look to get rid of their stake within 10 years, once a business has matured. In this case, the VC firm needs the money to invest in an up-and-coming soccer ball company. They suggest that Dale offer some stock to the public. After all, his brand is practically a household name, and many individual investors would love to be able to buy stock in the company. Plus, with the additional money the stock sale would bring, Dale's business will be able to expand internationally.

Dale agrees, so he hires an investment bank to arrange what's known as an **initial public offering**, or IPO. The investment bank, for a fee, helps draw up the terms of the offering—for instance, how many shares will be offered and at what price. Then, after they receive approval from the government, the shares are available to investors on a specified day. Often, favored clients of the investment banks will get the IPO shares since it's likely that the shares will experience immediate price appreciation once they hit the open market.

Many firms also prohibit their clients from "flipping," or quickly selling, IPO shares. Doing so isn't in the best interest of the company or of the market. People who do flip shares may find themselves left out of the next IPO placement, though it wouldn't be accurate to say that this is always how it works. There has been a good deal of writing and discussion about this in the wake of recent business scandals, and cases of abuse have been brought against major brokerage houses. A common scenario involves brokers giving out IPO shares to bigwigs of other companies in order to get them to have their own company's IPO through the same brokerage house. It's this "I'll scratch your back if you scratch mine" mentality that has caused so much distrust of Wall Street.

At any rate, once the new shares are offered to the public, they can be traded on a **secondary market**. In this case, we're talking about what's commonly referred to as the stock market. Before we get into how the stock market works, let's finish up with Dale, who by now has probably appointed himself CEO of the company. He may also be chairman of the board of directors, a group of internal and external (to the company) people who make important decisions about the direction of the company. Still, Dale has a lot less control over the company than he did when it was just his hands and his garage. However, he's also been able to grow the business and his personal fortune. After all, 33 percent of $20 million is a lot more than 100 percent of $200,000.

There's one other thing we should note about Dale's company. Even though it's now public, if he wants to expand further, he can always offer more stock to the public in a **secondary offering**, a follow-on offering of additional public shares, which may or may not initially be placed privately. Current shareholders are often upset by these offerings since their relative stake in the business is decreased. Of course, if Dale doesn't want to upset his investors, he has a number of other options for raising more money, including the issuance of bonds. We'll discuss that in detail in the chapters on bonds. For now, just be sure not to confuse the secondary market with a secondary offering.

The Stock Market

So, just what is a secondary market? Simply put, it's a place where investors can buy and sell their interests in investments that have been issued by another party. The stock market is just one of many secondary markets—there are others for everything from bonds to gold. Even what we commonly refer to as the stock market is actually made up of a number of different exchanges—usually physical places—that facilitate the trading of investments.

In America, the most famous of these is the New York Stock Exchange, or the NYSE. Stocks that trade there are said to be on the "big board," or "listed." Shares of many of the country's largest public companies, the so-called "blue chips" (taken from the highly valued gambling markers of the same name) are bought and sold on the floor of the NYSE.

"The floor," you ask? Although technology has allowed for many advances, the NYSE still maintains a central spot where buyers and sellers of stocks conduct business. However, not just anyone can walk out on the floor and start buying and selling stock. The exchange allows a certain number of "seats," each of which permits its holder, or a designated representative, to operate on the floor. A number of member firms control the seats and ensure an orderly trading environment. Their agents are known as **specialists**.

These agents are usually responsible for trading one or a few specific stock issues. Sometimes, more than one specialist will deal in a particular stock. It is the specialist's job to ensure that a stock's price remains in balance. To do this, the specialist retains an inventory of stock. For example, if a number of buyers suddenly emerge and no sellers are available, the specialist is required to sell some of the stock from inventory. In doing so, the specialist hopes to make a reasonable profit. Sometimes, however, maintaining an orderly market will require engaging in a losing transaction. Through sound judgment, the specialist attempts to make money for his firm over the long haul.

ACTION ON THE FLOOR

So how does an order actually get filled on the NYSE? Although specialists are the decision makers, a number of other people are involved in the action. Here's a step-by-step breakdown:

1. An investor places an order.
2. A brokerage firm checks the investor's account, provides pricing information, and enters the order. Then the brokerage transmits the order to the NYSE trading floor, via computer or phone.
3. The NYSE's computer system receives and stores the order, then transmits it to a specialist.
4. The order appears in the specialist's "book": a list of all pending orders.
5. A firm clerk gets the order and then passes along it to the firm's floor broker.
6. The floor broker takes the order to the trading post, where the stock is traded. The broker competes for the best price and then closes the deal.
7. A transaction report goes to both sides of the transaction.
8. The brokerage house is notified and the trade is settled—that is, paid for.
9. The investor is notified of the successful trade.

The American Stock Exchange, located not far from the NYSE, operates in much the same way as its neighbor. Ironically, that wasn't always the case. In fact, the American Stock Exchange was known as the "Curb Exchange" until the 1950s, because it was originally a place out on the street where traders would gather to swap shares of companies that weren't eligible for membership on the NYSE.

Now, shares in the smallest and least established companies trade on the Over-the-Counter (OTC) stock market. This market is also known as the "pink sheets," since the prices for stocks in the OTC used to be recorded on pink slips of paper. Stocks that trade on this market are often called "penny stocks," because many of their shares literally change hands for pennies.

The OTC market is regulated by its own governing body—the National Association of Securities Dealers, or NASD. Many stocks that get their start on the OTC eventually become established enough to get listed on a major exchange. However, many choose to continue to be traded directly through the OTC's big league—the Nasdaq, which is an acronym for the National Association of Securities Dealers Automated Quotation system.

The Nasdaq was widely watched during the tech boom of the 1990s. It was founded in 1971 as a virtual trading floor where members were able to buy and sell stocks directly over a network of computers rather than on a physical floor. Over time, the Nasdaq developed into the place where many high-tech firms chose to have their stocks traded. It is still home to many well-established firms, especially those in the technology and health-care fields. Stocks that trade through Nasdaq are bought and sold by **market makers**.

WHO ARE MARKET MAKERS?

Market makers differ from specialists since they compete with each other to fill orders placed by investors. To do this, market makers post the prices they're willing to buy (the "bid") or sell (the "ask" or "offer") stock at. The difference between these two prices is known as the spread. To make money, market makers hope to engage in a number of transactions, allowing them to pocket the spreads.

It's worth mentioning that in October 1998, the National Association of Securities Dealers and the American Stock Exchange merged. As a result, the Nasdaq and the ASE are now under one corporate umbrella. Each of the markets continues to function independently.

In addition to the national exchanges, there are many other specialized exchanges, including the Chicago Board Options Exchange (CBOE), which is where many options contracts change hands (more on these later). Also, many regional markets, such as the Pacific Stock Exchange and the Philadelphia Stock Exchange, continue to stand as physical trading floors electronically linked to their larger brothers. Although our focus is on American investing, we should note that there are a number of established markets abroad, such as the Tokyo Stock Exchange and the London Stock Exchange. While they operate somewhat independently of our markets, the buying and selling of stocks has truly become a global affair. It's common to hear about investors in Europe reacting to the activity on the NYSE, or vice versa.

Wall Streeters

Although we've been covering them in the text, here's a quick rundown of the major players on Wall Street:

INVESTMENT BANKERS are generally responsible for finding and structuring financing deals with companies. Often, their deals involve the issuance of stock.

SYNDICATORS, or people who work in syndication, are responsible for helping a company place its stock into the hands of investors, usually institutional investors. They often conduct "road shows," or presentations that highlight a company's merits.

TRADERS. This moniker covers a number of different groups, all of whom buy and sell stock. The first group consists of specialists and market makers who help keep their respective stock exchanges functioning properly by buying and selling shares to other interested parties. The second group includes professionals who buy and sell stock for their own organizations, either to fill in-house orders (sales traders) or to make their firm a profit (trading the firm's capital). Lastly, there are day traders, individual investors who trade in and out of stocks on a daily basis to make a profit.

BROKERS are sales agents who help clients buy and sell stocks.

MONEY MANAGERS are professionals who manage large sums of money for wealthy clients, institutions (pension plans, universities, organizations, etc.) or the gamut of funds available to investors.

ANALYSTS are responsible for researching stocks. Buy-side analysts help money managers make investment decisions. Sell-side analysts are responsible for generating research at brokerage houses and investment banks. Of course, there are also independent agencies that specialize in analyzing stocks, bonds, and other investments. Standard & Poor's is one such company. Many investors, even those with access to buy- or sell-side analysis, also use research from places like Standard & Poor's, which have no investment banking or brokerage businesses, and thus none of the associated conflicts of interest.

Stock Indexes

Most investors don't necessarily hear about the activity of a given stock exchange as much as they hear about the activity of the "market." What this usually translates to is the performance of one, or more, stock indexes. An index measures the overall performance of a number of stocks, which have been grouped together for the purpose of representing a particular segment of the stock market or the stock market as a whole.

The Dow

In 1884, Charles Dow, along with his partner Edward Jones, released a market average made up of 11 railroad companies. Back then, the railroad industry was running full steam ahead, and Dow reasoned that by looking at the performance of those companies, one could get a good idea of just how well the overall economy was doing. Afterward, he did a bunch of adjusting to the index, and by 1897 there were 20 railroads in the index. That same year, Dow Jones &

Co. came up with another index that followed the performance of 12 industrial companies.

Over the next 100 years, things were further adjusted and a third index for utilities companies was added. Taken as a whole, these three indexes—the Dow Jones Industrial Average, the Dow Jones Transportation Average, and the Dow Jones Utilities Average—form the Dow Jones Composite Average. It's worth noting, however, that "the Dow" you'll commonly hear about is the Dow Jones Industrial Average, an index comprised of 30 companies. To many people, the Dow continues to represent the blue chip stocks of the NYSE, even though it can contain stocks that trade elsewhere. For example, Microsoft and Intel, which both trade on the Nasdaq, were Dow components in 2002.

The S&P 500

Those looking for a broader window into the stock market usually look to the S&P 500. This index is comprised of 500 leading companies in the United States. Unlike the Dow Jones averages, the companies in the S&P 500 come from a greater number of industries. The "500" differs not only in its scope, but also in its construction, because it is a market-weighted index. What this means is that a constituent company's representation in the index is directly related to its size. Thus, the largest company in the index accounts for more of the index than the smallest. This is important in representing the economy as a whole, since the performance of a large company has a greater economic impact than that of a small company.

You might wonder what we mean by "the size" of a company. In this case, it has nothing to do with the number of employees that a company has. Rather, it depends on the company's **market capitalization**, or how much all of the company's stock is worth—that is, the number of shares outstanding times the current stock price.

While we're on the subject, it's worth noting that there are a few different categories for market capitalizations, or "market caps," as they're commonly called. Generally, companies that have market caps exceeding $5 billion are considered large-cap stocks. Companies with values between $1 billion and $5 billion are called mid-cap companies.

And companies worth less than $1 billion are considered small caps. Because of these designations, S&P has additional indexes that track the performances of small- and mid-cap stocks. The S&P SmallCap 600 index is made up of 600 small-cap companies, while the S&P Mid-Cap 400 index represents 400 mid-cap companies. We'll talk more about how these different types of stocks stack up later.

Another helpful way of approaching S&P's indexes is through the S&P/Barra indexes. These indexes take S&P indexes, like the "500," and divide them into two separate indexes—growth and value. The distinction between the two groups is solely based on a stock's book-to-price ratio, which measures the value of a company's assets against its current stock price. We'll discuss this ratio more in Chapter 5.

Other Indexes

Another common index, which does represent a particular stock exchange, is the Nasdaq Composite. The Nasdaq was the widely watched index during the late 1990s since it's a good indicator of how well technology stocks are doing.

There's also the Russell 3000, which is even wider in scope than the S&P 500. It tracks the 3000 largest companies in the U.S. The Russell 2000, a subset of the "3000," tracks the 2000 smallest companies of its big brother. And the Wilshire 5000, the last broad index, tracks practically every publicly traded stock in the country.

There are also a large number of other indexes out there, from those tracking the price of gold to those tracking the movements of stocks on the London Stock Exchange.

Using Indexes

In addition to their value as gauges of overall market activity and economic health, indexes are used by investors to provide benchmarks by which the performances of individual investments can be measured.

For example, someone who owns stock in a technology company might want to know how that particular investment is performing.

While calculating the return the stock has provided is fairly straightforward, the result doesn't necessarily mean much. What the investor really wants to know, more than simply, "How much did I make?" is, "How am I doing compared to other assets in this class?"

An easy way to check this would be to compare the performance of that particular stock to a fairly close index. In this case, the Nasdaq Composite would work well. Upon looking at the specific stock pick, the investor might only be up 2 percent for the year. However, if the Nasdaq has lost 3 percent that year, the investment has done well, relatively speaking. The key here is picking an appropriate benchmark. For instance, while comparing the performance of a small-cap stock to the S&P 500 would give you some indication of how well your investment has performed, it would be even better to use the S&P SmallCap 600 as your gauge.

You can find information on indexes in many places. Most news programs usually mention the daily closing prices of the Dow Jones Industrial Average, the S&P 500, and possibly the Nasdaq Composite. Your local newspaper should also provide these numbers. Financial publications like *The Wall Street Journal* contain information on a wide range of indexes, including some of the more esoteric ones.

There's one last important thing to mention about indexes before we move on: They are not investments in and of themselves. It might be easy to confuse the two since the difference is somewhat subtle. However, indexes are simply reflections of the price movements of actual investments. Ironically, it's possible to invest in something that looks to mimic an index by investing in all of the stocks that make up that particular index. For more information on these types of investments, see the chapters on mutual funds.

Common Stock Market Terms

Now that you understand how the stock market is measured, you might be wondering about some of the common terms people use when describing market movements.

Bull Market

This phrase became so ubiquitous in the 1990s that it would almost be strange if you hadn't heard it before. So, what is a bull market? In the broadest sense, it's a prolonged period of increasing stock prices. While there's no true definition of a bull market, it's generally thought of as a time when a major stock index (and usually more than one major stock index) increases by 20 percent or more. Of course, stock prices don't have to shoot straight up during a bull market. It's natural for days of rest during the process, as some traders take their profits, or disbelievers sell off their holdings. For an idea of what a bull market looks like, take a gander at Table 4-1.

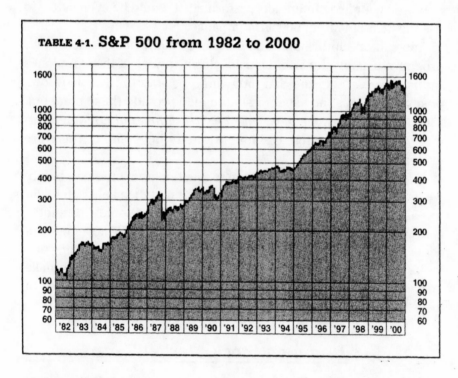

TABLE 4-1. S&P 500 from 1982 to 2000

Bear Market

As most people who have been through a number of market cycles can tell you, for every bull, there will be a bear around the corner. A bear market, like its nemesis, is hard to define. However, it is always a time when stock prices decline or remain stagnant over a long period. As in a bull market, the action isn't necessarily one-sided. In fact, it's natural for prices to rise for a few days, only to get squashed back down by a wave of pessimism. Such movements are known as "bear traps." This is also why you might hear people talking about a new bull market beginning only when stocks are able to "climb a wall of worry."

A classic bear market occurred in the 1970s. For a visual idea of how stock prices acted during that period, look at Table 4-2. As you can see, stock prices were pretty much in hibernation.

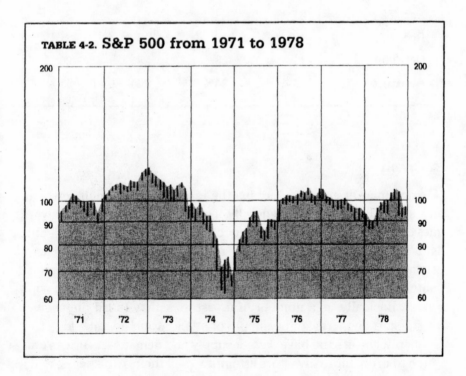

TABLE 4-2. S&P 500 from 1971 to 1978

Of course, when bear markets finally subside, stock prices tend to move up pretty sharply. Table 4-3 provides a historical account of how stock prices performed after the end of a given bear market.

TABLE 4-3. How The S&P 500 Performed After a Given Bear Market

Bear Market Ended	2 Months After	6 Months After	9 Months After	12 Months After
June '49	13%	23%	26%	42%
Oct. '57	1	10	19	31
June '62	14	21	27	33
Oct. '66	12	22	25	33
May '70	12	23	40	44
Oct. '74	8	31	52	38
Aug. '82	31	44	60	58
Dec. '87	13	19	18	21
Oct. '90	11	28	28	29
Average	**13%**	**24%**	**33%**	**37%**

A Crash

A stock market crash is perhaps the most dramatic occurrence an investor will experience. Generally, it's a quick and severe downward movement in stock prices, often occurring within a single day. Panic is ultimately the cause of a crash, and sometimes the initial reason isn't even clear. However, extremely high stock prices that don't match up with underlying economic conditions usually provide good tinder. Basically, as a number of investors scurry to rid themselves of stock, they increase the supply of stock available, thus lowering stock prices—it's the basic law of supply and demand. As prices continue to drop, more investors attempt to sell their own shares, and a vicious cycle ensues. The two most famous crashes occurred in 1929 and 1987.

Who Protects Investors?

After both the crashes of 1929 and 1987, the government created additional ways to protect against future crashes.

The Securities Act of 1933, passed after the crash of '29, was designed to better regulate the market. In addition, the Securities and Exchange Commission was created in 1934. The SEC, a government watchdog organization, continues to oversee our financial markets today and serves many functions in its efforts to protect investors.

One of the SEC's notable duties is to ensure that the trading of securities is done properly. To this end, the SEC requires people intimately involved with a company to regularly disclose their stock holdings, as well as their intentions to buy or sell additional shares. These people, often corporate officers or big investors, are known as "insiders." You've probably heard of the phrase "insider trading." While many insiders buy and sell stock in companies legitimately, there have been famous cases of abuse in the past. Because of this, the phrase has taken on a negative connotation.

MORE ON INSIDER TRADING

Most insider trading cases revolve around people buying or selling stock on information that wasn't publicly available at the time. The motive, of course, is profit. Because of their close ties with the company they're investing in, many insiders have access to news before it's released. That's why their ability to buy and sell stock is restricted. They sometimes choose to ignore these restrictions, but more often, insiders devise ways around the rules.

A recent example is the case of biotechnology company Imclone, in which the CEO of the company, Dr. Sam Waksal, learned that the FDA would be denying his company's request to market a drug. Before this information was released to the public, Dr. Waksal tipped off a number of friends and family members. As a result, many of them sold their shares beforehand. In doing so, they managed to get out of the stock before it plummeted upon the release of the news. Of course, insider trading can work the other way too. For example, if the FDA had decided to approve the drug, it would have proven profitable to buy the stock before the news was released.

Not that insider trading is limited to company CEOs. Many Wall Street analysts have been accused of receiving information before it was made available to others and then divulging this information to clients. Of course, there's a fine line between being a good researcher and receiving inside information. In an effort to help draw this line, the SEC passed a rule known as the Fair Disclosure Regulation, or Regulation FD. The regulation requires companies to disseminate important information universally.

The SEC also requires most publicly traded companies to submit a slew of reports to the agency, including quarterly and yearly performance statements. A bit later, we'll talk about how you can use these statements to research potential investments.

After the 1987 crash, additional steps were put in place to ward off future repeat performances. The NYSE added what is known as a "curb system," which automatically halts trading for an hour if the Dow Jones Industrial Average falls 250 points in a day. If it falls 400 points, trading is halted for an additional two hours. Although the system is generally aimed at giving frenzied investors a chance to rethink their actions, it was also intended to stem the bleeding caused by computerized trading programs, which are designed and used by large traders to buy and sell blocks of stocks based on prevalent market conditions.

Buying and Selling Stock

Now that you understand how the stock market works, you're probably wondering how you go about participating in it. The answer is, through a broker.

A broker is an organization, and often a specific individual representing the organization, that buys and sells stocks on behalf of individual investors. Brokerage houses generally make their money by charging a transaction fee for every share of stock they buy or sell for you; this is their **commission**.

There are a few different kinds of brokerage services:

FULL SERVICE brokerage firm, the traditional type of agency, offers clients a specific person to manage their accounts, along with other benefits like proprietary research. Of course, the commissions you'll pay at a full-service brokerage will probably be higher than those levied by other places.

DISCOUNT brokers are a cheaper alternative to full-service brokers. These firms usually provide their clients with simpler services, and their rates are much lower than those of full-service brokerages.

DEEP DISCOUNT brokers are great for investors who do their own research and make their own investment decisions. These firms charge the lowest rates, but provide only the most basic services of buying and selling stocks.

ELECTRONIC brokerage houses are typically discount brokers that allow their clients to manage their accounts online. Many also offer online research tools, and some have even begun moving toward the full-service model, offering investors a wide range of services for slightly higher fees. In turn, many traditional brokerages offer Web-based services to their customers.

Many brokerage houses are merely divisions of larger investment firms, which may also have investment banking divisions or additional trading operations. This is important since any advice you receive from a brokerage house may be somewhat influenced by these other operations.

For example, if a brokerage house is recommending a particular stock, you may want to find out if they currently make a market in the stock. In other words, they might have a vested interest in placing blocks of that particular stock into investors' hands. This is not necessarily bad. In some cases, it may be to your advantage. Still, it's always wise to investigate this issue before making a decision.

A larger conflict of interest concerns the research put out by brokerage firms. Some critics assert that a company's investment banking relationships might adversely affect the firm's ability to remain unbiased when conducting and disseminating research. Why? Well, since investment bankers are responsible for doing business with corporations, they may frown upon negative opinions put out by other departments within their companies. This doesn't necessarily mean that research from brokerage houses is bad. Many provide terrific information on the companies they follow. In some cases, a close relationship with the company can positively affect their ability to assess it as an investment. However, you should always seek more than one opinion before making any investment decision.

These issues probably have you wondering how you can go about finding a reputable brokerage house. The first step is deciding what level of service you're looking for. If you like the idea of having someone to help you along the way, you may want to go with a full-service broker. To refresh your memory on stockbrokers, revisit Chapter 3. If you're a do-it-yourselfer, a discount or online broker may be just your ticket. Either way, opening an account is relatively easy. It largely involves establishing your identity and depositing enough money to cover the initial purchases you want to make. If you're under 18, your account will have to be opened by a custodian of legal age. Online brokerages have made the entire registration process especially easy—in some cases, everything can be done over the Internet.

Although some people feel embarrassed about the amount of money they have to invest, you shouldn't let this concern you. Many exchanges and brokerage houses spend lots of money trying to reach smaller investors. Your business should be appreciated as much as the business of the firm's largest client. It's easy to be intimidated, but remember, you are the customer, and you are doing your broker a favor by choosing to do business there. Besides, a number of modest sums put together amount to a large chunk of change for an investment house. Also, many smaller investors become bigger fish over time.

There are a number of ways to find your broker. If you'd like to go with someone at a local office, your phone book should provide you with a number of options. You might also want to consult with friends who already have investment accounts. And there's always the Internet. Checking out a firm should be relatively easy. The NASD keeps tabs on all of them, and information about their recent activities, along with any complaints filed against them, is readily available.

Your new broker's role includes seeking to execute your orders at the best possible prices. If you wish, the broker will keep your stock certificates for you. This is known as keeping your stock in "street name." In most cases, keeping your physical certificates with your broker is advisable. Although they are replaceable, doing so can be a real hassle. In addition, should you want to sell your stock, it will be much easier if your proof of ownership is already at your broker's place of business. Your broker will also forward any payments you receive as a shareholder, or any correspondence that the company provides to its investors. In addition, money you've provided to your broker for future stock purchases will usually be held in some sort of short-term account, like a money market. Be sure to investigate your options, since many brokerages offer more than one choice.

Types of Orders

Once you've selected your broker, deposited some money, and (hopefully) done your homework, you'll probably wish to purchase some stock. Before you pick up your phone or log on to your broker's website, you should be familiar with the different types of stock orders you can place. Keep in mind, these different instructions have been designed to help clear up the possibility of a communication breakdown. They protect both your broker and you. Also, since some orders require more effort on the part of your brokerage firm, the pricing for each type of transaction will probably differ. Before you place an order, be sure you understand how much you'll be paying for the service. The common orders are:

AT THE OPENING tells your broker to buy or sell a given stock at the best price obtainable when the market opens.

AT THE CLOSE tells your broker to buy or sell a given stock during the last 30 seconds of a day's trading.

DAY ORDER is an order that is only good for the day on which it's given. If the order cannot be filled that day, it will automatically be cancelled.

GOOD TILL CANCELLED (GTC) is an order that remains open until it is either filled or cancelled. It differs from a day order in that it is not automatically cancelled at the end of a trading day. Other time limits may also be specified, such as "good this week."

LIMIT ORDER is an order to be executed at, or better than, a price specified by the customer.

MARKET ORDER is an order to be executed at the current price available to the broker immediately after its receipt. If not stated, an order is always considered a market order.

STOP ORDER is an order that doesn't go into effect until the actual market price reaches the price specified by the order. A stop order to sell, also known as a "stop loss," is placed below the stock's current price. It is designed to protect an investor from a sudden decline in price. However, because of the nature of the market, it's possible for the order to get executed at a price lower than that of the actual stop loss.

STOP LIMIT is a combination of a stop loss and a limit order. It instructs the broker to execute the trade at a given price, but adds another parameter signifying at what point the order should no longer be executed. The second parameter can be the same as the stop price. For example, a stop limit can specify a stock be sold at $30 (the stop part) with a limit of $25. In this case, if the stock cannot be sold between $30 and $25 (probably because the price has fallen too quickly), then the shares should no longer be sold. If the stop and the limit are the same (for instance, $30 and $30), the stock can only be sold at that price ($30).

When placing a stock order, it's important to remember that your broker is only required to do what you instruct. While it's your broker's role to execute your orders at the best possible prices available, there can often be some wiggle room in fulfilling this obligation. In addition, market forces can often interfere with your best-laid plans. For these two reasons, it's wise to make most of your orders limit orders. Doing so ensures that you'll pay or receive exactly what you planned for a given investment.

One other word of advice: It's best if you can get some type of written confirmation that your order has been received and understood. If you're conducting your transactions online, this should be automatic. However, if you deal with your broker over the phone, you might have to ask for some form of confirmation before the order is actually placed. Having a record of what you instructed your broker to do may become important in the event of an error or some other problem. It will also force you and your broker to define exactly what the order is. Here's a real world example of this:

Larry calls up his broker with some good news. He heard that one of his holdings issued a positive press release after the close of trading. Based on the favorable news, he expects the stock to increase in price the next day. He tells his broker, "Sell my shares if the stock jumps at the open." The broker agrees. The next day, the shares open up 50 percent amid heavy volume. However, within an hour or two they have come back down a lot. Larry calls his broker, only to hear that his shares were not sold during the time of higher prices. The broker claims that trading was so intense that he couldn't get the shares sold.

A while later, when Larry realizes that his broker makes a market in that particular stock, he becomes suspicious about the trade. He realizes that it's unlikely that his broker would have had trouble getting rid of a few hundred shares during the price spike. So he calls up the brokerage house and lodges a complaint. In response, the broker claims that no set order was ever placed. Without a record of the request, Larry doesn't have much of a case. Moreover, in a sense, Larry was at fault since his instructions to the broker weren't all that clear. Had he said, "Sell my shares if they hit $16," that would have constituted a limit order. By giving his broker vague instructions, his argument was pretty weak. Ironically, that one particular price spike proved to be a rare selling opportunity. Two years later, the stock had still never come close to the price it did on that day. Larry learned his lesson the hard way. And shortly thereafter, he dumped that broker too.

While this story isn't meant to scare you off from brokers or using the phone to place trades, it highlights the importance of being clear and direct when placing trades. It also proves that having a record of your instructions can sometimes prove useful. Notice that this also means you'll have to make your mind up about what you want your broker to do for you. While many brokers will gladly help you make your decisions, the best route is to decide what course of action you want to take *before* you get on the phone to place an order. Doing so requires research. We'll discuss this in the next chapter.

Summary

A stock represents partial ownership of a company. As a stockholder, you take on the same risks that all other business owners do—namely, that the company might cease to exist. However, as an owner, you also benefit from any success the company experiences. To purchase stocks, you'll probably go through a broker. To follow the stock market's performance, you should watch an index or two.

CHAPTER 5

Researching Stocks

Now that you know what stocks are and how they're bought and sold, you're probably wondering how to pick the good ones. In fact there are many different ways to gauge the attractiveness of a stock. Some people choose one method and stick with it, while others use a number of measures as checks and balances. While the latter is certainly recommended, you'll eventually settle on the methodology that works best for you. For now, a brief introduction into the basics of analyzing stocks will be helpful, as will some basic strategies that investors and traders employ.

Fundamental Research

As we explained in the previous chapter, a stock represents an investment in a company. So, the most basic way to gauge a stock's appeal would be to figure out how attractive its underlying company is. This sort of research is called **fundamental analysis** since it looks into the basic financial condition of a potential investment.

Generally, all the information you'll need to perform fundamental analysis is publicly available. This is because, as we mentioned earlier, all public companies in the United States are required to provide investors and potential investors with documents outlining their operations as well as their finances.

Of course, there are many different elements of a company that you can look at. You may choose to focus on one, a few, or many of these facets. Here are a few basic things you might use:

Earnings

The first, and arguably the most important, fundamental characteristic you should look at is a company's earnings. This refers to the amount of money a company generates after its expenses; in other words, its profits. A company's earnings are important because, as an investor, you're putting money into a business now in the hope of receiving more at a later date. Basically, this future profit will be based on a company's earnings, either in the form of dividends or from increases in the stock's price (which other investors have presumably been bidding up because the business has been generating healthy profits). This is why stock investors focus on a company's future earnings, and, because the future is difficult to predict, why they look at a company's earnings history in an effort to gauge how much its earnings might grow in the future.

On the surface, analyzing a company's earnings seems relatively easy—just find out how much it's been making, right? Unfortunately, there are a number of different ways of looking at a company's earnings. In fact, the term "earnings" itself represents myriad ways of accounting for profits. Moreover, some companies go in and out of profitability. Why? One good reason would be if a company's business is cyclical—that is, subject to periods of strength and weakness. For example, construction companies usually do very well when real estate markets are booming; they often lag when real estate sags. Thus, you would expect to see them produce solid earnings when people are buying houses.

Of course, the predictability of cycles and the earnings of cyclical companies is not always so clear cut. Consider a company that does a better job of controlling its costs during tough times. It would be likely to have better earnings than its counterparts. Also, keep in mind that some younger companies have yet to earn a profit at all.

So before you start investing, we should first discuss two different aspects of earnings.

THE TIMING OF EARNINGS

As we mentioned, there are two main time periods of earnings that you need to consider—past earnings and future earnings. Companies report their earnings on a quarterly basis, or four times a year, though the way companies keep track of time differs. While many keep time with the regular calendar year—their year starts on January 1—others have **fiscal years**, a type of business calendar that can start at the beginning of any month. Without getting too metaphysical, suffice it to say that no matter what schedule a given company keeps, you can expect to hear about the state of its business at least four times a year.

Now, there are a few ways of looking at a company's earnings history. The first would be to look at how much a company has earned in its last four reported quarters. This is known as **trailing earnings**, or earnings for the trailing 12 months (sometimes abbreviated as TTM). Looking at earnings this way gives you a good idea of how well a company has been doing most recently, and it avoids the hassle of worrying about what type of calendar it uses.

Another way of looking at earnings is by calendar year. This can get tricky if a company keeps a fiscal calendar. If that's the case, you're better off just following your company's fiscal calendar. But realize that trailing 12-month earnings can present a different picture than a company's earnings for a given year (calendar or fiscal), especially if a company has had a particularly strong quarter that is unlikely to be repeated. Also, within certain industries one quarter may be much stronger than another due to seasonal demand. For example, the back-to-school and holiday seasons are usually strong for retailers.

All of this may sound more confusing than it is. The point is to always look at a company's earnings history within the context of its business. Also, when comparing the earnings history of two or more companies, be sure that the periods you're looking at are comparable.

As far as future earnings go, you have a few main sources of information. Many companies regularly issue their own earnings guidance—an estimate of what they expect to earn in coming quarters. While some companies tend to be optimistic in their forecasts, others are known for being conservative. Because of this, it might prove useful to look at how close a given company has come to its guidance in the past. You can do this by digging up old estimates and comparing them with the numbers actually reported.

Professional analysts are another source of earnings estimates. Many analysts take a company's guidance and then apply their own gauges to arrive at their own numbers. Others rely solely on their own methods, which may include field research, historical data, and a little intuition.

When taken as a whole, the average estimate of professional analysts is known as the **consensus estimate**, or the "Street" estimate. This number is largely treated as the basic target a company must hit. A lot can also be learned by looking at the consensus estimate versus a company's guidance (if available)—you can often get a sense of whether people are optimistic or pessimistic about a company's near-term future.

One other source of earnings numbers, extremely popular in the late 1990s, is the so-called "whisper numbers." These numbers, which can be found all over the Internet, are supposed to be unofficial estimates from people intimately familiar with a company, such as executives. While you shouldn't put much credence in whisper numbers, they're sometimes interesting to watch.

QUALITY OF EARNINGS

Knowing when and how a company reports its earnings is just the beginning, though. An even more important issue is just what type of earnings a company is reporting. This is because the term *earnings* encompasses many different accounting animals. You might recall that a short while ago we said earnings are the money a company gets to keep after it pays off all of its expenses. Well, they are ... sort of. The problem is, not all earnings are created equally. Without getting into too many accounting nasties, let's look a little deeper.

When a company calculates its earnings, it generally has a number of different items to add and subtract along the way. For instance, say a company has a bunch of equipment in its factories. Every year, the equipment gets older and its value decreases. This is called *depreciation*. When figuring out earnings for a given year, a company can treat this depreciation in more than one way. Companies may also include or exclude other items, like money paid for taxes. But it gets worse. If a company offers its employees a pension plan, there are many ways that it can treat the interest it earns on the money in the retirement pool. And if it issues its employees **stock options**—contracts that give them the right to purchase stock in the future—it has yet another item that can be treated in more than one way. (We'll discuss stock options in Chapter 6.)

One last common sticking point is a credit or debit against earnings that occurs because of some special circumstance, or the **onetime item**. An example of a credit would be the sale of a large asset. If a company decides to sell off its hamburger manufacturing operations, for instance, it can expect to get paid a lump sum of money. While the company isn't likely to see another gain like this at the same time next year—unless it sells off another business—the money it made is certainly money earned. And on the debit side, a company might settle a large lawsuit during the course of the year, which forces it to pay out a large sum of money. While the likelihood of a similar charge next year is small, the money is still a real amount that had to be paid.

The point is, so far as an investor is concerned: When a company includes a onetime item in an earnings calculation, it's easy for people to get the wrong idea about how well that company is growing its earnings.

As you can see, finding out just how much a company has actually earned can get pretty complicated. But fear not—there are certain standardized ways of reporting earnings.

Here are some of the more popular versions:

AS-REPORTED EARNINGS is the most traditional way to look at earnings. An as-reported earnings number includes all charges except those related to discontinued operations, the impact of cumulative accounting changes, and extraordinary items. These earnings are figured under generally accepted accounting principles (GAAP).

EARNINGS BEFORE INTEREST, TAXES, DEPRECIATION, AND AMORTIZATION. As the name suggests, this number tells you how much a company has made before it counts a bunch of accounting items. While companies love to dish out things like

EBITDA, you shouldn't place too much emphasis on them because, for one thing, the EBITDA doesn't factor in the money a company has to pay in yearly taxes. While some other items can certainly be ignored, taxes *must* be paid for a business to stay in operation. To the investor, there's no point in relying upon numbers that don't take things like taxes into consideration.

PRO FORMA EARNINGS are used in the case of a major structural change to a company, such as a merger. They are used to describe what a company's earnings "would be like." Although they can be helpful in certain circumstances, the fact that they exclude many items makes them susceptible to abuse.

OPERATING EARNINGS. As an investor, what you should be most concerned with is how much a company is making with its core business or businesses, its operating earnings. This measures profits from a company's principal operations. It excludes corporate or onetime expenses.

CORE EARNINGS. Unfortunately, there has been a lot of confusion over exactly how operating earnings should be calculated. As such, the numbers aren't 100 percent reliable. To help investors sort out this mess, Standard & Poor's has developed its own system of calculating what it calls "Core Earnings." These are basically a measure of how much a company's real businesses are earning. To arrive at this number, Standard & Poor's excludes pension income, interest costs, and goodwill, which includes things like the value of a brand name, a premium paid for an acquired company, and other similar intangible assets. Among other things, S&P's Core Earnings includes stock option expenses and restructuring charges.

Using Ratios to Value Stocks

Okay, so what do you do with earnings numbers once you have them? It's really not that helpful to have numbers in a vacuum. For this reason, there are a number of common ratios that investors use to put various financial data into a usable context. Some of the more common ratios are profiled below.

P/E RATIO

Perhaps the most common measure of a stock is its price to earnings ratio, or **P/E ratio** for short. As you might have guessed, the P/E ratio is calculated by dividing a stock's price by its per-share earnings for a given year. If Company XYZ is expected to earn $2.30 per share in the coming year and its stock is currently selling for $46 a share, the shares of XYZ are trading at a P/E ratio of 20.

Notice that in the example above, we calculated the P/E based on a company's expected earnings, meaning an earnings estimate. This is called a **forward P/E**. Some investors opt to use a company's trailing 12-month earnings instead, since that number is certain. While this isn't necessarily wrong, you're probably better off sticking with the forward P/E because it is designed to provide a snapshot of how much of a premium other investors are willing to pay for a company's future earnings; a higher ratio indicates higher hopes for continued earnings growth. In other words, investors are paying a lot of money based on today's earnings in the hope that future earnings will make the current price they paid look like a bargain.

While it's not a foolproof way of gauging a stock's value, the P/E ratio is a good place to start. It's most helpful when compared against other P/E ratios.

You might first look at a stock's historical P/E range—how high and low its P/E has been in the past. You might also compare it with the P/Es of other similar companies (just make sure the earnings are from similar time periods and of similar quality). You may also compare the P/E ratio of a particular stock to the P/E ratio of a market index like the S&P 500. You can calculate the P/E of an index by using the same process you use for an individual stock—look up the estimated earnings for the index and divide it into the current price. These comparisons will let you know just where a particular stock stands against its own history, its peers, and the broader stock market.

Note that P/E ratios can be industry specific, based on the characteristics of that particular group. For example, homebuilders and financial companies typically trade at below-market P/Es since their businesses are fairly mature. Also, keep in mind that just because a stock has a relatively low P/E doesn't mean it's worth purchasing. Other investors may be aware of a looming problem and discounting a company's shares accordingly. In fact, a low P/E can be either a good or bad sign. You'll need to do more digging before you know the full story.

EARNINGS GROWTH AND THE PEG RATIO

Next, you might want to look at how quickly a company's earnings have been growing over the past few years. To do this, simply take a company's yearly earnings results (make sure all the numbers are of the same type—for example, fiscal as-reported earnings) and subtract them from the next year's earnings. Once you have that number, divide it by the earnings number you subtracted. The result, once you move the decimal point over two places, will be the percentage of earnings growth that year.

If Company XYZ earned $1.00 in fiscal 1997 and $1.30 in fiscal 1998:

$$\$1.30 - \$1.00 = \$0.30$$

$$.30/1.00 = .3$$

Thus, in fiscal 1998, Company XYZ grew its earnings by 30 percent

After you've done this for a few years in a row, you can get an average annual growth rate, which gives you a better idea of a company's long-term performance.

Sticking with the same example, let's say Company XYZ earned $1.65 in fiscal 1999 and $2.00 in fiscal 2000. Using the formula from above gives us growth rates of 27 percent in 1999 and 21 percent in 2000. By adding the three growth rates and dividing the sum by three, we can get the average annual growth rate. For the three years, Company XYZ posted an average annual earnings growth rate of 26 percent.

Keep in mind that a company can experience no growth, or even negative growth, for one or more years. Also, note that trying to do this with a company that has an especially erratic earnings history won't prove too useful. And, companies whose businesses are more mature usually post slower earnings growth than their younger counterparts. Of course, their earnings also tend to be more consistent.

Once you have a company's earnings growth rate, you can get the **PEG ratio**, which can also be **helpful** to an investor. The PEG ratio is a company's P/E ratio divided by its growth rate, usually a projected growth rate.

If Company XYZ, from our example, is currently trading at a P/E ratio of 20 and has a projected three-year average annual growth rate of 27 percent, its PEG ratio would be 20 divided by 27, or .74.

By adding a company's recent earnings history into the equation, the PEG ratio provides you with a bit better picture of a stock's current valuation. In general, a PEG ratio under 1 is a positive sign, though as we said earlier, you should require more than a favorable ratio to compel you to purchase a stock.

SALES GROWTH AND THE PRICE-TO-SALES RATIO

A less common measure of a stock's value is its **price-to-sales ratio**. Like the P/E ratio, it uses a stock's current price as the starting point, but it divides the total value of all stock outstanding by how much revenue a company has in a given year. For example, if a company's common stock has a total market value of $1.5 billion and the company has $1 billion in annual revenue, its price-to-sales ratio would be 1.5. However, as with all of these ratios, the price-to-sales ratio should be looked at in conjunction with other factors.

Why? Well, for one thing, investors are likely to place a higher value on revenues that lead to greater profits or revenues that are growing rapidly. Also, if a company has a sizable amount of debt that will be paid out of its revenues, this will likely be reflected in a more moderate price-to-sales ratio. In addition, because of the differences in the ways various businesses operate, the average price-to-sales ratio of a particular industry may vary greatly from that of another industry. For that reason, you should only compare the price-to-sales ratios of similar companies.

BOOK VALUE

All of the measures we've been discussing have been based on a company's expected growth, whether in sales or earnings. But what if a company were to close its doors tomorrow? Surely, future growth expectations would be of little consolation, and even less value, for shareholders.

For that reason, it's also helpful to figure out how a company's current stock price relates to the sum total of its assets. This ratio is known as the **price-to-book ratio**. The divisor of this ratio is a company's **book value**, or its total assets minus its total liabilities: in other words, how much a company would have left after selling off all of its possessions and after all its loans have been repaid. A company's book value can differ from its **tangible book value**, which only counts things that have concrete values—like buildings, machines, desks, and, of course, any cash on hand. Tangible book value excludes hard-to-value items like patents.

To calculate a company's price-to-book ratio, simply divide its current stock price by its book value. While most companies will probably be trading above their book values, occasionally you may find one that isn't. Stocks that are trading at a discount to book value fit the classic definition of *undervalued*. However, as always, there may be something going on behind the scenes. Be sure to learn more before making a hasty decision.

OTHER KEY RATIOS

So far we've looked at a few valuation ratios, which gauge how fairly a stock is priced relative to some underlying fundamentals. There are other ratios that quantify a company's operating success or financial well-being. Like valuation ratios, these don't tell you much when they're standing alone. It's more helpful to compare them with a company's historical ratio, or those of its peers. Here are a few financial ratios you might use to evaluate companies:

CURRENT RATIO. This defines the relationship between a company's current assets—those that are relatively liquid or likely to be converted to cash within the next year—and its current liabilities—payments due within the next year. In essence, the current ratio lets you know whether a company is likely to pay its bills in the near term. This ratio becomes particularly important for companies with financial troubles. For many companies, having at least 1.5 times as much in current assets as in current liabilities indicates sound financial health, while a much lower ratio might signal an imminent cash crunch. However, a healthy current ratio will vary depending on the industry.

GROSS MARGIN measures how profitably a company is able to manufacture its products. Essentially, it is gross profit (the difference between a company's revenues and the cost of goods sold) divided by revenues. Gross margin is expressed as a percentage. The cost of goods sold usually includes items like the materials used in the products as well as the labor costs involved in the manufacturing process. In general, the higher the gross margin, the better. But keep in mind, a lot of other costs can stand in the way of solid profits.

LONG-TERM DEBT-TO-TOTAL CAPITAL. This ratio sounds complicated, but you can obtain it from a company's balance sheet. It's long-term debt divided by total capital, which equals shareholders' equity plus long-term debt, and is often expressed as a percentage. Its significance can be conveyed by looking at how big a homeowner's mortgage is to the value of their house. If a mortgage were close to the house's value, you'd wonder about that person's ability to maintain their place, right? Similarly, companies that are capitalized with more than 50 percent debt (a debt-to-equity ratio of 1:1) should be approached cautiously; they're running the risk of being too dependent on debt. If that's the case, the significant interest costs of all those loans might hinder future earnings, or make obtaining additional funds for expansion more difficult. Of course, certain types of companies can better manage higher debt levels since their incomes are fairly steady, just as a person with a steady, high-paying job would be better able to handle a big mortgage. Many utility companies, for instance, have traditionally been able to operate with greater levels of debt.

RETURN ON ASSETS and **RETURN ON EQUITY.** The first number, return on assets (ROA), is arrived at by taking a company's net income and dividing it by its average total assets. The second, return on equity (ROE), is equal to net income divided by average total common equity. These two ratios indicate how profitably a company is investing funds from stock offerings, borrowings, and retained earnings. When a company is using its borrowed money—known as *debt leverage*—effectively, its return on equity should be higher than its return on assets.

Dividends

There are still other ways of gauging a stock's attractiveness. For companies that pay dividends, you might look at past payment history. To reiterate, a dividend is a payment made to stockholders on a regular basis, and it usually represents a portion of a company's earnings. While many young companies don't yet pay dividends, others have been paying dividends for decades without interruption. Such a strong history suggests an extremely stable investment. More conservative investors, especially those looking for a steady income from their stock holdings, should take a long, hard look at a company's past history of paying dividends. Some of the longest dividend payers are listed in Table 5-1, on pages 81–82.

In addition to simply paying dividends, you should be on the lookout for companies that have steadily increased their dividends over time. This is because a steadily increasing dividend suggests that a company's business has continued to grow. Also, if the dividend continues to increase, an investor will be rewarded with an even greater **yield on cost** in the future.

How does this work? When you purchase a stock that pays a dividend, your yield is the amount of the annual dividend divided by the share price. For example, if you purchase one share of XYZ for $40, and the stock offers an annual dividend of $1.40, your yield would be 1.4/40, or 3.5 percent. However, if five years from now the stock

TABLE 5-1. Longtime Dividend Payers

Company	Cash Dividends Paid Each Year Since:	Dividend Increases In The Past 40 Years	Sector
3M Co	1916	40	Industrials
Abbott Laboratories	1926	35	Health Care
ALLTEL Corp	1961	37	Telecommunication Services
Altria Group*	1928	36	Consumer Staples
AmSouth Bancorp	1943	34	Financials
Anheuser-Busch Cos	1932	39	Consumer Staples
Archer-Daniels-Midland	1927	32	Consumer Staples
Automatic Data Proc	1974	29	Industrials
Avery Dennison Corp	1964	36	Industrials
Bank of America	1903	36	Financials
Bard (C.R.)	1960	36	Health Care
Becton, Dickinson	1926	38	Health Care
CenturyTel Inc	1974	29	Telecommunication Services
Chubb Corp	1902	28	Financials
Clorox Co	1968	30	Consumer Staples
Coca-Cola Co	1893	40	Consumer Staples
Comerica Inc	1936	39	Financials
ConAgra Foods	1976	32	Consumer Staples
Consolidated Edison	1885	31	Utilities
Donnelley(R.R.) & Sons	1911	36	Industrials
Dover Corp	1947	37	Industrials
Emerson Electric	1947	40	Industrials
Family Dollar Stores	1976	27	Consumer Discretionary
First Tenn Natl	1895	31	Financials
Gannett Co	1929	35	Consumer Discretionary
Genl Electric	1899	35	Industrials
Grainger (W.W.)	1965	33	Industrials
Heinz (H.J.)	1911	38	Consumer Staples
Household Intl	1926	40	Financials

TABLE 5-1. (continued)

Company	Cash Dividends Paid Each Year Since:	Dividend Increases In The Past 40 Years	Sector
Jefferson-Pilot	1913	36	Financials
Johnson & Johnson	1944	40	Health Care
Johnson Controls	1887	29	Consumer Discretionary
KeyCorp	1963	36	Financials
Kimberly-Clark	1935	34	Consumer Staples
Leggett & Platt	1939	33	Consumer Discretionary
Lilly (Eli)	1885	38	Health Care
Lowe's Cos	1961	40	Consumer Discretionary
MascoCorp	1944	40	Industrials
May Dept Stores	1911	31	Consumer Discretionary
McDonald's Corp	1976	27	Consumer Discretionary
McGraw-Hill Companies	1937	35	Consumer Discretionary
Merck & Co	1935	38	Health Care
Nucor Corp	1973	30	Materials
PepsiCo Inc	1952	35	Consumer Staples
Pfizer, Inc	1901	39	Health Care
PPG Indus	1899	37	Materials
Procter & Gamble	1891	40	Consumer Staples
Regions Financial	1968	32	Financials
Rohm & Haas	1927	38	Materials
Sigma-Aldrich	1970	28	Materials
Stanley Works	1877	37	Consumer Discretionary
Supervalu Inc	1936	36	Consumer Staples
Target Corp	1965	34	Consumer Discretionary
TECO Energy	1900	40	Utilities
U.S. Bancorp	1930	35	Financials
VF Corp	1941	35	Consumer Discretionary
Wal-Mart Stores	1973	29	Consumer Discretionary
Walgreen Co	1933	31	Consumer Staples

Cash payments based on ex-dividend dates from January 1– December 31 of each year.

*Formerly Philip Morris Cos

is still trading at $40, but the dividend has been increased to $2.00, the yield on your initial cost would now be 5 percent. To better illustrate the point, here are two real-world examples:

In 1991 the average price of Paychex, a provider of payroll and human resources services, was $0.96 a share (this figure has been adjusted for stock splits). Ten years later the company was paying a dividend of $0.44 a share! Obviously, during that decade, Paychex managed to significantly grow its business. However, an investor who had purchased the shares back in 1991 would be getting a yield on cost of over 46 percent at the end of 2001.

AmSouth Bancorp, a regional bank, provides a more realistic, yet still impressive, example. In 1991 the company's stock was selling for about $5.00 a share (again, split-adjusted). In 2001 the stock price was over $18.00. However, during that 10 years, the company also raised its annual dividend to $0.88. Thus, investors who purchased the stock in 1991 were getting a 17 percent yield on cost at the end of 2001. In addition, their stock had also more than tripled in value!

As you can see, stocks that consistently increase their dividends can reward investors handsomely, through both capital appreciation and rising income. However, be aware that even companies with long dividend histories sometimes fail to continue their stellar performances indefinitely. Two recent examples of longtime dividend payers who stopped making payments are Xerox and Corning. Both companies had been paying dividends for over 50 years before suddenly stopping their payments in 2002.

Throughout the 1980s and 1990s, the number of dividend-paying stocks steadily declined. As you can see in Table 5-2, in 1980, 93.8 percent of the companies in the S&P 500 index paid a dividend. In 2001, only 70.2 percent of "500" constituents were paying a dividend.

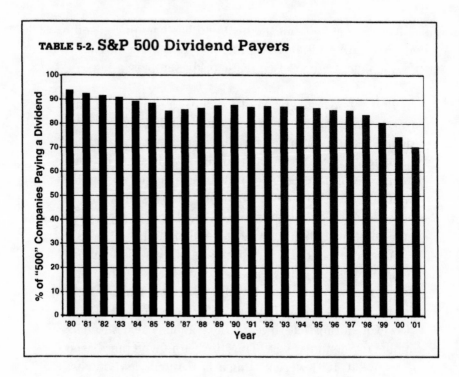

TABLE 5-2. S&P 500 Dividend Payers

However, that's not to say there aren't new dividend payers on the horizon. Companies that don't currently pay dividends may begin to do so as their businesses mature. For instance, in 2003, Microsoft announced that, for the first time, it expected to pay an annual dividend. Be on the lookout for companies that have recently begun or may soon begin to pay dividends. They're likely to be attractive stocks for long-term investors.

Technical Analysis

While fundamental analysis is the generally accepted approach to analyzing investments, there's another important way to study stocks: **technical analysis**, often referred to as TA. Although many investors remain skeptical of the value of technical analysis, it shouldn't be cast aside as useless pictorial voodoo. When combined with fundamental analysis, it provides a greater understanding of the attractiveness of a potential investment. This is not to say that you should solely base your investment decisions on technical analysis; however, you may find that it will give you a better idea of when to buy a stock or when to sell it.

The basic philosophy behind technical analysis is that the stock market represents a large body of investors and their informed opinions on stocks, and thus everything about an investment—including all of the fundamental analysis—is already reflected in a stock's current price. According to technical analysts, a stock's price is the sum total of investors' perceptions about that given stock. As such, all one has to do is look at the various aspects of a stock's price movement to ascertain what its future moves are likely to be.

Notice that technical analysis involves looking at "aspects of a stock's price movement," not simply a stock's price. By this, we mean that, in addition to examining a stock's actual day-to-day price movements, technical analysts look at things like volume. In most cases, they will also be doing a comparative study—that is, comparing a stock's action to that of another stock, an index, or something else.

Charts

If fundamental analysis is a number cruncher's dream, technical analysis is perfectly suited to someone with a visual bent or someone more interested in the psychological aspects of investing. This is not to say that technical analysis doesn't rely on numbers—it does. However, it tends to use underlying data in what some would argue is a more accessible way—namely, through stock charts. Table 5-3 is an example of a basic stock chart.

As you can see a stock chart is a basic graph with an X-axis and a Y-axis. For most graphs, the X-axis represents the time period being used and the Y-axis represents the price. Thus, the points that make up the line being charted are the various price points that a stock has traded at during a particular time.

There are many different periods that can be used, including prices by the minute, the day, or the year. One of the most common methods is using daily prices. That's how Table 5-3 was constructed. More specifically, it's a "bar graph," with the bars representing the price

TABLE 5-3. S&P 500 Price Index

range that the stock traded at during that particular day. The line through the bar indicates the stock's closing price on that day. One other variation you'll often see is the "candlestick chart." These types of charts take the bar graph one step further by also indicating whether a stock closed up or down during a given day, depending on the color of the candlestick.

VOLUME

Sometimes, charts will include another section below the X-axis, usually a simple bar graph representing the volume, or number of shares traded, for each day. Adding a volume measure is a good way to give a chart another dimension—it helps put the price changes in context by letting you know whether the movements occurred under normal circumstances. Often, you'll find that large jumps or slides in a stock's price happen on higher-than-average volume. In addition, looking back at the headlines from those particular days will usually yield some explanation of what caused the movement. You might then begin looking at whether the company is still operating under the same circumstances.

Using charts as a starting point for further inquiry is a good example of how technical analysis and fundamental analysis can work together to give you a more coherent investing picture. Table 5-4 is a chart with volume activity below it.

Just as there are many different pieces of fundamental data to look at, and an even greater number of ratios derived from that data, there are many different measures within the realm of technical analysis.

TABLE 5-4. **Stock Chart for Microsoft, with Volume Activity Noted Below**

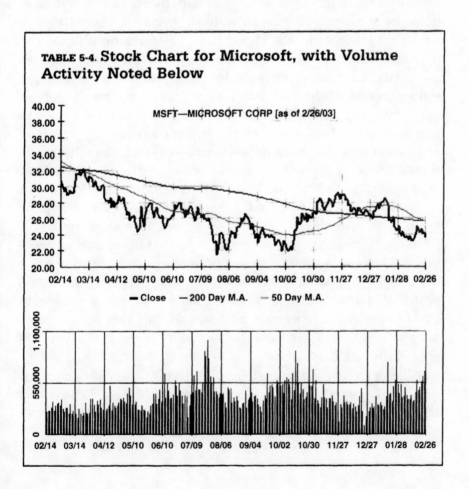

In truth, the preponderance of technical analysis is complicated and thus beyond the scope of this book. However, some of the more common methods are both useful and easily applied to a potential investment. Below, we'll discuss a few of the most basic technical concepts you're likely to encounter in the investment world.

SUPPORT AND RESISTANCE

The notions of support and resistance are straightforward, and you'll often hear them mentioned by market pundits. In a sense, they reflect psychological forces at work in the market.

When someone says a stock has "strong support" at a certain level, they mean that by looking at a chart, the stock seems to have had a lot of purchasing happen within a tight price range before it moved on to higher levels. This is known as **forming a base**. The thinking is that once a large number of investors have bought shares around a certain price, psychologically, they won't be interested in selling their stock for less than they paid. In fact, many investors might even purchase additional shares if the stock comes close to that level again. Thus, the stock has strong support.

Resistance is the opposite of support on a stock chart. It's represented by a level at which investors seem willing to sell their shares, or at least a level where they refuse to buy additional stock. The particular spot on a chart where this happens is often called a **top**. As can be seen in Table 5-5, the S&P 500 formed a classic top in 2000.

In most cases, you'll find that once a level of support or resistance is breached, it becomes its opposite. In other words, a stock that breaks through previous resistance will likely find future support at that level, and vice versa. It's not uncommon for stocks to trade in patterns like **double bottoms** for this very reason. Also, keep in mind that the second bottom isn't always at the identical spot of the first one.

Although there are no certain rules, levels of support and resistance do frequently surface. In some respects, the phenomena may be a self-fulfilling one; still, understanding the basics might better help you set short-term expectations for your own stocks.

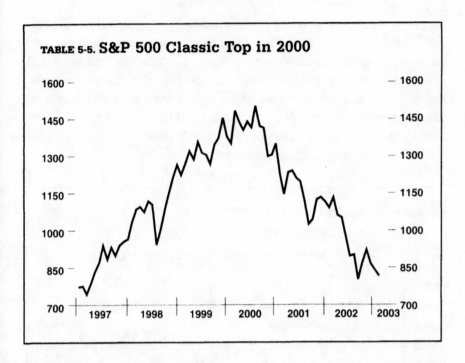

TABLE 5-5. S&P 500 Classic Top in 2000

MOVING AVERAGES

Technical analysts are especially interested in looking at a stock's price movements over a specific period of time. In most cases, they do so to determine whether a stock has been experiencing positive or negative momentum. This momentum is often referred to as a stock's "trend."

It's long been an accepted rule that a stock going up tends to continue going up, while a stock going down continues to go down. This might be because the stock's fundamentals continually get better, or because many investors "chase performance" by throwing their money into investments that have recently been doing well. Whatever the cause, technical analysts are always interested in stocks whose momentum has been departing from a recent norm.

To determine such deviances, technical analysts look to moving averages: an extrapolated line that provides a smoothed-out representation of a stock's recent pricing trend. By placing a moving average on the same chart as a stock's actual price movements, you can get a sense of continuance or divergence. While the two lines will always be snaking around each other, technical analysts are especially interested in instances when the moving average goes well above or below its typical position. In most cases, they assume that a sudden move in one direction will be followed by an even greater move in the same direction.

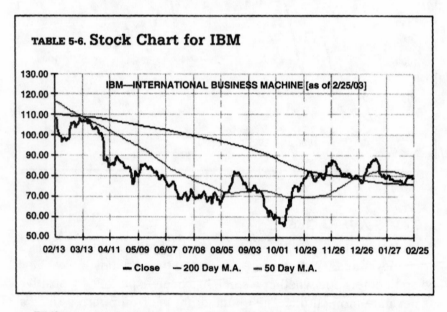

TABLE 5-6. Stock Chart for IBM

Different technical analysts favor different moving averages. Table 5-6 shows a chart with 50-day and 200-day moving averages. (The longer the period, the smoother the moving average will look.)

GAPS

We've demonstrated that charts will often show times of rapid increases and decreases in a stock's price. In most of these cases, the chart will have what is known as a "gap." While many people define gaps differently, they are essentially spaces between closing and opening prices indicating significant price changes that happened without purchases along the way. For example, the next day's opening is higher or lower than the previous day's close.

While gaps need to be taken in the larger context of a chart, many technical analysts find them interesting since they often signify a strong force in the market. In many cases, traders will look to the point of a gap as another form of support or resistance, and many will look to trade around the gap getting "filled." What this means is that many traders believe that at some point activity will occur in the gap area. You'll often hear people who believe that "every gap gets filled." Whether or not that's true, you might look at gaps as another interesting feature to study.

There are many ways to use technical analysis in making your investment decisions. Hopefully, the few examples above have at least given you a better idea of what technical analysis is about. If you're interested in learning more, there are a number of good books on the subject. For some ideas, check out the resources in the appendix.

Research Pitfalls

Before we finish our discussion on researching stocks, it might be useful to talk about a few ways *not* to make your investment decisions:

1. Don't act on "tips." It's likely that at some point along your investing path, you'll encounter someone who has a hot stock tip for you. The person might be a friend, a relative, or a broker. However, no matter who gives you the tip, you're better off seeking a second opinion and doing some research on your own.

2. Don't just look for extremely high yields or extremely low P/Es. While it's possible for a great stock to be trading at a lower-than-average P/E, or for a stock to offer a remarkably high yield, you should always approach such issues with caution. Many times, a stock's P/E is a reflection of some stated or latent issue going on with the company. Likewise, a high yield is often a reflection of

a depressed share price, which may also indicate some sort of problem. More important, a high-yielding stock will often see its dividend cut or dropped, especially if the underlying company is short of cash.

3. Don't purchase a stock just because you work, or worked, at the company. It's admirable, and often advantageous, for investors to purchase stock in a company they're familiar with. In many cases, they will have firsthand knowledge of its situation and may even get the stock at a discount. However, there are also risks involved. The primary risk is that putting too much of your money into the company you work for cuts down your diversification and leaves you vulnerable if something bad happens. For example, if you have your retirement money in company stock and the company goes bankrupt, you may find yourself unemployed and without your savings. Also, your view of the company might be overly optimistic. This is not to say that you shouldn't take stock options or invest small amounts in a company you work at. Just make sure you don't place all of your bets on the same horse.

Summary

There are many different ways to evaluate a stock. Fundamental analysis involves looking at the company behind a stock to see if it's in good financial shape. Technical analysis, on the other hand, entails looking at charts and graphs to figure out where a stock may go next. However, you shouldn't rely on just one measure to assess a stock— most successful investors evaluate a potential investment in a number of different ways.

CHAPTER 6

Stock Strategies

There are a tremendous number of stock-buying strategies. Many of them build upon the basic fundamental and technical analysis methods touched upon in the previous chapter. While it would be impossible to cover them all, we'll present a few of the most popular approaches in this chapter. Keep in mind, these strategies aren't necessarily exclusive—many can be used in combination. And all of them should be combined with some of the techniques we've already discussed. One last thing to remember: No matter what strategy you choose to employ, the key lies in staying true to the ground rules you lay out for yourself.

Value Investing

Value investing is a classic example of how an approach can be developed from fundamental analysis. It involves purchasing stocks that are considered undervalued by one or more fundamental measures. Although this sounds simple enough, determining the criteria for an undervalued stock is the subject of much debate.

It has been the case that a stock is considered undervalued when it trades at less than the sum total of its assets—that is, it's trading below its book value. However, few investors continue to abide by that definition. Their rationale is that companies are no longer the stodgy manufacturing firms they once were, that they're less likely to have large plants and raw materials that are easily valued. Instead, proponents of new valuation methods argue that in our technological age, intangibles like intellectual capital (a smart and capable work force) don't appear on a balance sheet. Proponents of this theory use

[93]

other valuation methods, such as the P/E ratio, to determine whether a company is undervalued.

The term "value," by the way, shouldn't be tossed around lightly. As the tech stocks collapsed in 2000, many self-proclaimed value investors were quick to point out that stocks were becoming undervalued simply because their prices were decreasing. Of course, just because an item is on sale doesn't mean that it's worth the discounted price. The truth is, most of the real value investors eschewed the high-flying technology stocks as they rose *and* as they fell, because their valuations never made them bargains.

Growth Investing

Growth investing has often been considered the antithesis of value investing because growth investors focus on how quickly a company has been growing, rather than on how closely its share price reflects its current value. As we touched upon earlier, measuring a company's growth usually involves figuring out how quickly it's been increasing its earnings or revenues.

Of course, successful growth investors don't just look to purchase the companies that have been experiencing the fastest growth. Instead, they look for companies that are experiencing growth at a reasonable price (GARP). To determine this, they might use a measure like the P/E to growth ratio discussed in the last chapter.

The main risk with investing in growth companies is the possibility that their growth may not continue in the future. As such, it might be wise to look at companies with long histories of strong performance, not just companies that have had one or two strong quarters. In general, growth investing tends to be slightly riskier than value investing; however, the potential gains will likely be greater too.

Buy What You Know

The "buy what you know" approach to investing is actually a way of finding potential investments rather than a pure investment strategy. However, there are investors who have built their portfolios around this philosophy. Buying what you know involves investing in companies that you or people you know do business with.

This approach, widely espoused by renowned investor Peter Lynch, posits that even the small investor has a powerful means of discovering solid investments: their eyes and ears. For the record, Lynch ran Fidelity's Magellan Fund from 1977 to 1990; over that time period, the fund was up 2700 percent.

Here's how it works: Let's say you decide to try a new department store in your area. Upon arrival you notice that the parking lot is packed with cars. Inside the store, the checkout lines are brimming with shoppers. And much to your liking, the prices are pretty good. Such an experience might prompt you to do a little more digging into the company. If you like what you see, and the company is publicly traded, you may even decide to purchase some stock.

Another example of buying what you know would be purchasing stocks of companies that operate within your area of expertise. For instance, if you're a pharmacist, you might be adept at picking good drug stocks. Or if you're interested in cars, you may be better than average at investing in auto stocks.

As with any strategy, there are a few risks. The first is that just because you happen to like a particular business doesn't mean that it will be welcomed by a larger audience. This is a caution to always investigate further before buying a stock. Also, your portfolio should remain diversified, with extra attention to ensure that all of your stock holdings aren't too closely related to your occupation. As discussed, if an entire industry turns sour, having all your income and investments in one place could prove disastrous.

CAN-SLIM

The CAN-SLIM strategy is another take on investing through fundamental analysis. It was created by William J. O'Neill, founder of *Investor's Business Daily*, a financial newspaper. CAN-SLIM is an acronym that stands for the seven criteria O'Neill suggests investors look for when choosing stocks: The *C* stands for current earnings. According to the CAN-SLIM method, investors should look for companies that have shown increasing earnings versus what they made in the same quarter of the previous year. This is commonly known as year-over-year earnings growth. This particular facet of the strategy should come as no surprise, since investors place a high priority (and a high share price) on companies that demonstrate strong earnings momentum. Just be sure that the earnings growth isn't a one-time event.

Although it's an offshoot of C, O'Neill also says investors should focus on a company's annual earnings, represented by the letter A. Specifically, he recommends that investors be on the lookout for companies that have seen their annual earnings per share increase in each of the past five years. In a sense, this will assure you that a company's strong growth isn't a recent fluke.

The third letter, N, stands for "new." The idea here is that a potential investment should differentiate itself from the crowd in some way. For example, the company might have recently introduced a new product, or perhaps it recently came under new management. Whatever the case, there should be a catalyst for future growth on the horizon. Many times, a hot product or a fired-up CEO is just what a company needs to break out of a rut or to further its success.

There's one other "new" you might wish to consider: a new price high. Many investors look for stocks that are trading at or near an all-time high. While this seems to go against the "buy low, sell high" axiom, many studies have shown that stocks reaching new highs often continue to go even higher.

The S stands for supply and demand. O'Neill posits that investors should also concern themselves with how many shares of a given stock are currently outstanding. This is because a stock's ability to rise and fall in price is directly related to how much of it is for sale. A stock's daily trading volume further affects its price volatility. In the ideal situation, according to the CAN-SLIM method, a stock should have few shares outstanding and fairly heavy daily volume. These two factors will allow its price to increase more rapidly.

L represents the concept of "leaders and laggards." As an investor, you should only concern yourself with companies that are leaders in their industries. Buying lesser companies because their share prices are cheaper is generally not a sound strategy. While there's often room for more than one company in a given market segment, the leader usually enjoys a number of advantages over its lesser competitors.

O'Neill also believes that investors should focus on institutional ownership, or I, before they purchase a stock. Institutional investors manage large amounts of money for things like pension plans and university trusts. Institutional support for a stock is big plus since these investors often plunk down big bucks over time. As a smaller investor, you stand to benefit if their purchases move the price higher.

Lastly, M stands for market direction. What this means is that investors should be mindful of the larger market, especially its over-all direction. While some stocks perform strongly even during severe downturns, it may be difficult for you to fight the trend. In some cases it may be prudent to put your money elsewhere until things look better.

We've spent a decent amount of time explaining the CAN-SLIM method because it offers a lot for you to think about. For some, it provides a specific way to approach investing—a seven step program that is clearly defined. You may instead wish to approach it as a number of different facets to consider when looking at potential invest-ments. And in any case, CAN-SLIM makes the valid point that investors should look for leading companies with good products, good management, and good earnings.

Market Timing

We've purposely put market timing as the next investment strategy since you just read about it as the CAN-SLIM's M. Market timers try to anticipate price movements and aggressively buy and sell based on their forecasts. While it's possible to use different timelines—such as daily movements or multiyear cycles—most market timers use technical analysis as their way of predicting the movements. Some are very successful at it; however, novice investors are probably bet-ter served by a strategy like dollar–cost averaging.

A subset of market timing is daytrading. This concept came to the forefront in the 1990s, when seemingly everyone knew someone who was daytrading. It involves the rapid buying and selling of stocks, with all activity usually occurring within a single day, and is a concept many people have thought about: Since stocks move up and down throughout the day, why not just buy some, wait for a little move up, and then sell? This is precisely what daytraders attempt to do. But it's not easy, and the commissions and taxes that are involved with buying and selling stocks make it even more difficult to consistently earn a profit. In short, a longer-term approach to investing is both easier to digest and more likely to produce favorable results.

If you still insist on trying to time the market, consider this observation by S&P's Howard Silverblatt, an expert at conducting quantitative studies, who looked at daily price changes in the S&P 500 from 1928 through 2002: The first day of the month is most likely to be an "up" day, the second day of the month is the next likeliest gainer; alternatively, the 18th of the month is the likeliest "down" day and the 19 is the second likeliest "down" day. In addition, by summing up all of the days in a given month, Silverblatt discovered that July has the highest incidence of being "up," while February had the lowest chance. Take a look at the results of the study, in Table 6-1 . . . pretty cool stuff.

Dogs of the Dow

The Dow dividend strategy, also known as the "Dogs of the Dow," is a straightforward way to invest in stocks. At the end of every year, you simply buy the 10 highest-yielding stocks from the list of 30 stocks that make up the Dow Jones Industrial Average, putting the same amount in each. You then hold these 10 stocks until the next year, at which point you repeat the process, keeping those that remain in the list and selling off those that don't. With the proceeds, you purchase the newcomers.

Historically, this strategy has worked well, even during overall market weakness. The real strength of the strategy is that it forces you to buy depressed stocks and sell them when they're high. You'll also find other variations on this same basic strategy, and many of them are worth looking into.

TABLE 6-1. Want to Time the Market?

Day of Month	% of Days Up	% of Days Down	Sum of Days	% of Months Up	% of Months Down
1	58.65%	38.71%	January	53.47%	45.18%
2	58.16	40.12	February	48.97	49.10
3	57.16	40.99	March	50.67	47.07
4	51.92	45.74	April	52.01	45.56
5	55.19	43.57	May	51.04	46.99
6	52.19	45.85	June	52.08	46.25
7	48.23	50.38	July	54.27	43.37
8	50.15	47.61	August	51.19	47.01
9	48.73	48.58	September	50.19	47.81
10	52.75	45.77	October	50.64	47.51
11	52.21	45.66	November	53.12	45.33
12	48.16	49.12	December	52.63	45.09
13	49.10	48.65	**Average**	**51.70%**	**46.34%**
14	51.72	46.19			
15	55.22	42.99			
16	53.81	44.54			
17	55.01	43.80			
18	46.57	51.79			
19	46.77	51.88			
20	51.19	46.87			
21	47.21	51.13			
22	47.80	50.00			
23	48.94	48.94			
24	52.83	45.33			
25	47.01	51.16			
26	51.63	46.82			
27	50.83	46.28			
28	53.53	44.48			
29	50.65	47.10			
30	55.03	42.19			
31	57.52	41.42			
Average	**51.70%**	**46.34%**			

Dollar Cost Averaging

Dollar cost averaging is arguably one of the safest and most powerful methods of investing. It involves investing a fixed amount of money into the same stock or stocks on a regular basis. For example, you might choose to invest $200 in five stocks ($40 in each) every month.

The secret behind dollar cost averaging is that you establish a position in a stock over a long, steady period of time. During that time, the stock's price will likely fluctuate. By investing a set amount every month, you actually benefit during the stock's periods of weakness. How? Because for the same amount of money, you can buy more shares when the price is depressed. As long as the stock's price increases over the longer term, you'll make out well. In fact, even if the stock's price doesn't go up, your risk is still greatly diminished with this strategy. Consider the following example:

On October 31, 1929, Gigi starts dollar cost averaging $100 per month into the Dow (while this wasn't possible back then, there are now mutual funds that track indexes . . . for more on them see Chapter 10). Over the next 10 years, the Dow's performance is atrocious—on a monthly basis, it closes higher only three times. In fact, by the end of 1939 it has lost 46 percent of its value. Keep in mind, this was during the Great Depression, a horrible economic period. And yet, despite the horrible conditions, Gigi has managed to eke out a 5 percent return over the 10 years. While this is certainly not a spectacular 10-year return, it's not bad considering the conditions. The secret to Gigi's success was that he was buying shares when they were even lower than the minus 46 percent finish over those 10 years (many times during the period, the Dow closed at less than 100). More important, 20 years later Gigi's investment would have been worth a fortune.

Despite dollar cost averaging's effectiveness with investments that are generally trending downward, it's still best applied to high-quality stocks. Many investors select a diversified list of fairly conservative stocks and then dollar cost average over a period of many years. In general, the stocks do quite well over the long run and, just as important, the investors also sleep quite well at night. That's the other beauty of this strategy: Once you set it up, it virtually runs itself.

Bottom Fishing

Bottom fishing is a term you'll hear mentioned from time to time. Essentially, bottom fishers look to buy shares that have been badly beaten down, usually through a sudden and sharp drop in price. In some cases bottom fishers may be value investors looking for stocks that have reached attractive valuations. In other cases, they may simply be buying the shares in anticipation of a short-lived price rally that often occurs after a steep sell-off. No matter what the reason, bottom fishing is a risky proposition because there's usually something behind a stock's fall. However, it's true that in many cases the selling has been overdone.

While bottom fishing is a strategy best left to fairly experienced, aggressive investors, you shouldn't rule out the possibility that one day a stock you like will fall for one reason or another. If that ever happens, you'd be smart to investigate the cause of the weakness. If the problem seems temporary, or the market seems to have overreacted, don't shy away from purchasing the shares. After all, making sound, independent decisions is what investing is all about.

Reinvesting Dividends

As we've discussed, some companies choose to return a portion of their profits back to their shareholders in the form of dividends. In turn, some shareholders choose to reinvest their dividends into the companies that pay them out.

This cycle of collecting and reinvesting dividends can be a profitable one. Why? Because of the investor's best friend: the compounding effect. In the case of reinvested dividends, the results are even more impressive, since all of the components—the stock price, the number of shares held, and sometimes the dividend—tend to increase over time.

As you've probably guessed, the longer you follow this strategy, the greater the effect is likely to be. Because dividends are paid on a regular basis, this strategy also serves as a form of dollar cost averaging; however, many investors also choose to continue dollar cost averaging more shares on their own in addition to the reinvestment of dividends.

Just how powerful can dividend reinvestment be? Consider Table 6-2.

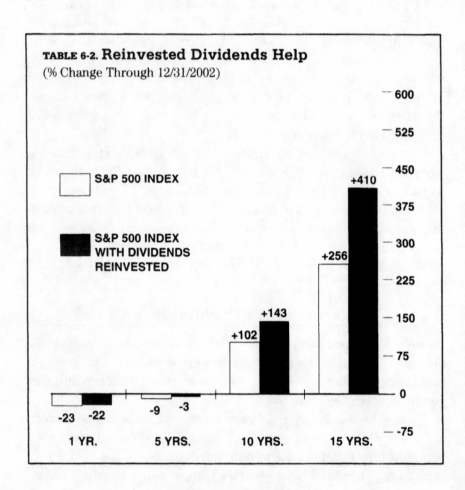

TABLE 6-2. Reinvested Dividends Help
(% Change Through 12/31/2002)

The chart shows the returns from the S&P 500 versus returns from the same index with dividends being reinvested along the way. While the difference isn't significant over a short period of time, after 15 years reinvested dividends made a tremendous difference in performance.

To make things even easier, many companies also offer their own dividend reinvestment plans, or DRIPs, which allow investors to automatically reinvest the dividends they collect. Beyond the obvious time savings, DRIP investors are often able to get the additional shares at little or no additional cost. In other words, they don't have to pay broker fees. They do have to pay taxes on the imputed income from the dividends, though.

More than 800 public companies offer such plans. They generally don't charge investors a fee for joining their plans, and some companies even allow investors to reinvest their dividends at a discount to the prevailing market price (ranging from 1 to 10 percent). Moreover, many DRIPs also allow investors to purchase additional shares without an intermediary—that is, without commissions. While in most cases you'll need to buy at least your first share from a broker, a number of companies now permit you to buy even the first share directly from them.

Why would companies make reinvesting dividends so easy? Mainly because additional share purchases, especially from long-term investors, benefit them too. Many dividend-paying companies, like banks and utilities, need a large amount of capital to conduct their businesses, and DRIPs are an easy way for them to raise additional funds. In the end, reinvesting dividends is a win-win for both investors and the companies they invest in. One other thing to note is that many mutual funds also allow investors to reinvest their dividend payouts. (For more on mutual funds, see Chapter 10.)

Summary

There are many different stock strategies floating around out there. Some, like dollar cost averaging, are designed for maximum efficiency and minimum effort. Others, like daytrading, are high-stakes games that become full-time jobs. Ultimately, you'll have to decide what your own investment philosophy is. Just know that it's okay to either use one of the strategies outlined here or one of your own.

CHAPTER 7

Advanced Stock Concepts

While no book can cover the entire world of stock investing—especially not a guide for beginning investors—we can certainly touch upon a few advanced concepts that are commonly talked about by everyone from market pundits to cocktail party conversationalists. You might use this section as a start toward learning more about complicated investing strategies, or simply as a way to impress your next dinner guest. You will at least find the concepts interesting food for thought.

Options

It's important to understand stock options not only because of their value to investors, but also because they have become a more prominent form of compensation in the workplace. Simply put, options are contracts that permit their holders to either buy or sell an underlying asset (like a stock) at a given price during a specified length of time. Options that allow investors to purchase stock are known as *call* options, while those that allow investors to sell stock are called *put* options. Most, if not all, options granted by companies to their employees are call options.

Options Basics

Options actually fall into the larger category of **derivatives**, or investments constructed from "real" underlying investments. This is not to say that options aren't real investments. By holding an options contract, you simply have the *right* (but not obligation!) to purchase or sell the underlying investment for a particular price; however, you do not yet possess that investment.

In addition, as an options holder you do not have any of the rights given to shareholders of the underlying stock. For example, you don't have voting rights or receive dividend payments. You can only reap these benefits if you purchase the underlying stock.

One important thing to understand about options is that they offer their holder a certain amount of **leverage**. By leverage, we mean that for a given amount of money, an investor can control an asset worth a larger amount. As you'll see, for a small price, options give an investor great power.

So, just how do options work? Basically, there are a few components to any options contract. The first is the **strike price**. This is the price at which you're able to buy or sell the underlying security with a given option. Strike prices are predetermined and remain fixed throughout the option's life. Options with a number of different strike prices are spaced either 2.5, 5, or 10 points apart, based on the underlying stock's price.

The second component is the **expiration date**. After this date, the option becomes worthless. For American options, the expiration date is always on the third Friday of a given month. Thus, an option with a May expiration date must be used by the end of trading on the third Friday in May. Although most options have expiration dates within a few months of their issuance, LEAPS, or Long-term Equity AnticiPation Securities, are options with expiration dates up to 39 months away.

Finally, there's the price of the option itself: how much you must pay to own it. Options prices are generally quoted for the price of one share, though an options contract usually represents 100 shares. In other words, if the listed price of a call option is $1.00, to purchase one contract it will actually cost you $100. While the methodology behind options pricing is complicated, simplifying the process yields two major factors: the **time premium**, or amount of time left until expiration, and the underlying stock's price volatility.

Options can be bought and sold through exchanges just like regular stocks. In fact, many brokers now offer options trading as an additional service to their customers. Although there are two main types of options contracts, there are many different ways to play the options game. Most investors choose to purchase either *puts* or *calls* based on the belief that the stock's future price will make doing so favorable. When a stock's current price makes an option's strike price attractive, the option is said to be "in the money."

For example, if you're holding a call option with a strike price of $30 and the stock is currently trading at $35, your option is "in the money." The same would be true of a put option with a strike price of $40. In turn, if you were holding a call option with a strike price of $30 for the same stock, your option would be "out of the money." And when an option's strike price matches the price of its underlying stock price, the option is said to be "at the money."

Investors holding an "in the money" option have two ways of booking their profit. They can look to sell their option to someone else or they can **exercise** the option. Exercising an option means that the options holder is choosing to take advantage of the right bestowed by the contract. However, to do so the holder will have to either commit more money to purchase the underlying stock (in the case of a call) or already own the stock (in the case of a put). More important, when exercising an option, be sure that the sum total of the trade will be profitable. For instance, an "in the money" option might not necessarily be profitable when exercised. This is because the initial purchase price of the contract is part of the total amount invested. Consider the following example:

Johan buys a May call with a strike price of $60 on XYZ stock. The contract costs him $6 a share, or $600 total. Later, the stock's price reaches $65 a share. Johan decides he might like to exercise the option since it's "in the money." However, he should first consider what his profit would be. To do this, he'll need to add the cost of the options contract to the cost of the stock. Thus, by exercising the option, he'd actually be paying $66 a share— more than the stock's current price. In addition, he hasn't even included the commissions associated with purchasing the investments. In this case, Johan would be far better off selling the option to someone else instead of exercising it himself.

It's true that the simplest options strategies involve buying and selling options as investments in and of themselves. Perhaps the best part of such strategies is that the risk is always clearly defined: You risk the amount of money you paid for the option.

However, there are many other ways to use options. Another popular, and safe, method is to use options as insurance for your existing stock holdings. For instance, if you're concerned that one of your investments might report unfavorable earnings in two weeks, which would surely sink the stock price, you might consider purchasing a put contract for a price close to the current one. Doing so would protect you from much of the downside if the stock falls. And again, your only risk would be the amount of money that the option costs. Here's an example of how it might work:

Ryan owns 100 shares of company XYZ that he purchased for $60 a share five months ago. The shares have had a tremendous run and are now trading at $95 each. However, the company will be reporting its fourth quarter earnings in two weeks, and it's possible they will miss the consensus estimate. Ryan doesn't want to prematurely sell the shares outright for a number of reasons, a main one being because he'll then be saddled with a higher tax payment. Besides, if the report is good, the stock may even continue to reach new highs.

However, Ryan also doesn't want to see the stock price fall significantly below its current level. In the end, he decides to purchase a put option with a strike price of $90. This contract gives him the right to sell 100 shares of XYZ at $90 each, even if the stock is trading well below that price.

By purchasing the contract, Ryan preserves most of his gain and limits his downside to a loss of $500 (plus the amount that he paid for the contract). If the stock continues to go up, he can either sell the option contract to someone else (probably for less than he paid) or let it expire, in which case he only loses what he paid for it. If the stock goes down, he can either sell the put for a profit (it would be "in the money") and keep his stock position, paying taxes only on the gain from the put, or he can exercise the put and sell his stock position as described earlier.

Where Options Come From

By now you might be wondering where options come from in the first place. Well, they come from other investors who are willing to take the other end of the bargain that an option represents. This is known as "writing" an option. The most common, and safest, way of writing an option is the **covered call**. This involves writing a call option on a stock you already own.

In other words, you create a contract that says you'd be willing to sell your shares at a specified price (usually higher than the current price). Why would you do this? Again, for insurance. However, in this case you'd be betting that the stock's price will remain somewhat stagnant for the life of the option. In the worst scenario, your stock would get "called away," meaning the purchaser of your option chose to exercise it, forcing you to sell your shares at the specified price. But even in that case, you'd presumably be getting a fair price for the stock, plus the amount you sold the option for. In the best case, the option would expire and you'd collect the premium, or the price of the option. Writing covered calls is an especially useful tactic when the market seems to be stuck in a rut.

A riskier options strategy involves writing **naked calls**. As you can probably guess, the "naked" refers to the fact that an investor is writing an option on an underlying stock that is not owned. Therein lies the danger: Since a call allows another investor to buy a stock at a particular price, and because a stock has no theoretical top price, someone selling a naked call is exposed to a limitless loss. In short, writing naked calls is not for inexperienced investors.

Naked puts, however, are a slightly more conservative strategy. By writing a naked put, you are only "exposed" to a loss equal to the difference between the put's strike price and zero.

Employee Stock Options

So, what about the stock options doled out by companies? These are basically call options that allow their holders to purchase a set amount of stock at a set price. In many cases, however, they will have a vesting period. In other words, their holders will have to wait for some amount of time before they can exercise the options. Most of these options will be issued at a price below the current value of the underlying stock; however, some may be issued at higher prices.

The idea behind stock options is that they give employees an incentive to work harder, since their own fortunes will be more closely aligned with those of shareholders. While this is often true, there's a hidden danger for employees receiving stock options: There is no guarantee that they will ever be worth anything. For this reason, it's advisable for employees to never consider options as anything more than icing on the cake.

Futures

Like options, **futures** are contracts that allow their holder to buy or sell a specific investment. However, futures are **obligations**—in other words, there is no option to exercise them. When they expire, everything must be settled with cash. Futures are most closely associated with **commodities**—products like coffee, pork bellies, and orange juice. If you've ever seen the movie *Trading Places*, you already understand how this works:

Say you think that coffee producers are going to have a tough time with their crops this year. That would mean that prices for coffee beans would go up (since the supply will be low). To profit from your belief, you could purchase a coffee futures contract, which would lock in the ability to purchase coffee at a particular price. Thus, if prices go higher in the future, you come out ahead.

Also, like options, futures contracts are leveraged investments—the amount you pay for them allows you to control a much larger underlying investment. This means that for a small amount today, you may be able to reap large profits later. Of course, it also means that if you end up sitting on the bad side of the contract, you may be forced to come up with a lot more money to finish off the trade.

So, you ask, how does this relate to stocks? The answer is: Mainly because futures are also available on things like stock indexes. An investor, for example, can purchase a contract on the S&P 500. These futures amount to bets on where the S&P 500 will be on a future date. The difference between the contract's specified price and the real price is the profit or loss. Some investors pay close attention to the action surrounding these futures contracts, since it indicates the current beliefs of relatively savvy investors.

In truth, futures are not well-suited to most investors, especially beginning ones. However, watching them can provide some insight into the market's psychology.

Margin

Another way for investors to use leverage is **margin**. In the brokerage world, a margin account is one that lets an investor buy additional stock based on the amount of money and stock already in an account. In other words, margin is a loan collateralized with the assets already in a brokerage account. Like any other loan, an investor on margin must pay a certain percentage of interest to the brokerage house, with the amount varying according to a number of different factors.

There is no doubt that margin can be an alluring, and profitable, tool. Unfortunately, it also goes against the common wisdom bestowed earlier in this book: that you don't get rich by getting in debt. Yes, opening a margin account allows you to buy even more of those stocks that you've thoroughly researched and fully expect to appreciate. However, it also does a few other things.

First, it starts you off in the hole. Since you are effectively using borrowed money to invest, your returns will have to be even greater to compensate for the amount of interest you're paying. If you remember the section on credit cards, this probably sounds familiar. But buying on margin has another danger—the possibility of a **margin call**.

Since your brokerage isn't expected to watch you lose the entire amount of money you've been loaned, they have the right to phone you up when times get tough. What they'll tell you is something like, "Put more money in your account or else."

"Or else what?" you ask.

Or else they'll sell off the stock you bought on margin and possibly the other stocks in your account.

That's right—by entering into the margin agreement, you give your broker the right to liquidate your other stock holdings if your margin position is in bad shape. So, not only are you forced to get rid of a lagging stock at an inopportune time, you also may be forced to sell other perfectly good stocks when you don't want to. And there have been instances when even that wasn't enough to pay off the losses accumulated on margin. People have lost houses playing the margin game.

Repeat this mantra: "If I don't have the money to invest, I shall not invest."

One interesting side note about margin is that it often causes a dropping market to continue its descent. This is because as investors get margin calls on their falling stocks, they're often forced to sell other stocks. This in turn starts a vicious cycle of selling and more margin calls. In fact, after the stock market crash of 1929, the federal government tightened the rules surrounding margin accounts. In essence, the amount of money a person could borrow was restricted. Before then, people pretty much borrowed as they saw fit.

Shorting

So far we've been talking about making money as investments increase in value. So, who makes money when stocks go down? People who are **shorting** stocks.

In essence, selling a stock short, or shorting, involves borrowing shares of stock at a given price in the hope that they will soon fall. Then, when they do, the person who is shorting, known as a "short," is able to buy the shares back at a lower price to replace the borrowed shares. The difference between the two prices is the profit.

Many people, especially the typical investor who is "long" in the market, have a particular distaste for shorts. This negative sentiment is only heightened by the fact that short sellers are often vocal in expressing their views on the companies they're shorting, in an effort to entice more investors to sell their stock, which would push the price down even further. Some proponents of short selling argue, meanwhile, that the role of short sellers is important since they help weed out weaker companies in the marketplace.

Whether or not you buy the argument, you shouldn't take short selling lightly. It comes with substantial risk. As we previously pointed out, a stock, at least in theory, has unlimited upside. Since shorts are betting against that potential, their relative downside is theoretically unlimited. In other words, if you bet that a stock will go down and it actually triples, you will be out a great deal of money. However, even if you're right, your maximum profit can only be as great as the price of the stock when you began shorting it. You also run the risk of getting caught in a **short squeeze**.

The short squeeze occurs when a large number of shorts all attempt to close out their positions by purchasing shares at the same time, effectively creating a vicious cycle of higher prices and greater losses for their short positions. What's worse is that short squeezes often happen when a stock has already shown strong price movement. Thus, the short squeeze only adds fuel to the fire for other long investors who haven't yet purchased shares. Stocks that are thinly traded are prime candidates for short squeezes, since there are few shares available in the first place. Should you ever decide to short a stock, try to stick to issues with large daily volumes.

One other question that commonly comes up when discussing short selling is: Who are the shorts borrowing their shares from in the first place? The answer is pretty simple: from those longs that haven't told their brokers not to lend out their shares. In other words, most of them.

That's right. If your broker holds your shares, they can actually be loaned out to short sellers—the very people working to undermine your investment. However, you reserve the right to tell your broker that your shares should not be loaned out. Not that loaning them out is of any particular risk to you. The broker can require a short to "repay" the loan if it seems to be getting out of hand. And as we mentioned above, many times a bad move by the shorts further boosts a stock's price.

After-Hours Trading

We've already discussed how stock markets work—that they're places, either physical or virtual, where people buy and sell investments. What we didn't mention is that stock markets, in the United States, at least, usually have "regular business hours." For example, the NYSE stops trading at 4:00 P.M. Hey, even traders have to sleep, right? Well, not if they don't want to.

Because of technological advancements, changes in the culture of Wall Street, and just plain old investor enthusiasm, the late 1990s saw a rise in the popularity of so-called "after hours" trading platforms. While professional investors had been placing trades past 4:00 P.M. for quite some time, individual investors were finally given the same opportunity. Of course, with this new opportunity also came risk.

Without getting into the gory details, after-hours trading is essentially a pure marketplace, where buyers and sellers transact directly with each other. Generally, very few shares of a particular stock trade hands after hours, so the spreads are wider. In some cases the after-hours price will reflect a development that has occurred after the close of regular trading, such as an earnings announcement. In other cases it will simply reflect someone trying to rip someone else off.

For most people, after-hours trading is kind of pointless. It comes fraught with all sorts of risks, and probably with higher commissions to boot. And usually the opening price the next day will be similar, or more advantageous, than the price the night before. If anything, you should look at after-hours prices as a possible indicator of the next day's action, but not as the place to make your own trades.

Summary

Although many of the concepts covered in this chapter aren't recommended for beginning investors, all investors should be aware of what they are and how they work, since market commentators often mention them, and, more important, because they can provide valuable insight into just how large and complex the stock market is.

PART 3

Bonds

CHAPTER 8

What Are Bonds?

B onds are a strange breed. While many investors will name a savings bond as one of the first investments they ever held, very few understand how large and complicated the overall bond universe is. In fact, to many, bonds remain an enigma.

The basic premise of bonds is pretty simple: They're IOUs between a borrower and a lender. Both governments and corporations borrow billions of dollars a year from individual investors, and bonds are a common way for them to do so. Like a savings account, the initial amount borrowed is called the **principal**, while the lender is generally paid in the form of interest. And bondholders, like stockholders, can also be rewarded by appreciation in the price of bonds they hold.

There are two main types of bonds: those issued by government agencies and those issued by private companies. We'll discuss the varieties in both categories.

Government Bonds

As the name suggests, government bonds represent loans taken out by a government agency. People are often surprised to hear that even the federal government needs to borrow money. In fact, every day, citizens are constantly loaning huge sums of money to Uncle Sam.

[119]

Treasuries

U.S. government securities include Treasury bills, notes, and bonds. Treasury bills are short-term obligations, usually with 13-, 26-, or 52-week maturities. They're sold by the government through auctions. Bills are usually offered in a minimum denomination of $10,000. Higher denominations are available in $5000 increments: $15,000, $20,000, etc.

These bills sell for less than their face value—"at a discount"—with the investor paying the full amount at the maturity date. In this case, the difference in values represents the interest payment for the loan.

Series EE Savings Bonds

Another type of government bond that follows this pattern is the Series EE savings bond. These bonds are also issued at a lower face value, with the holder getting paid in full when they mature. Many investors get their first taste of bond investing through a Series EE bond since they're often given as gifts to young children. This is primarily because they're a safe investment with a firm payout date.

The main difference between Treasury notes and bonds is the length of time it takes them to mature. Notes may take up to seven years to mature, while bonds can have maturities ranging from 5 to 30 years. Beyond their safety, U.S. government securities have another attractive feature—their tax treatment. Usually, they aren't subject to state or local taxes, although Uncle Sam still takes his cut.

Zero Coupon Bonds

Zero coupon bonds are similar to the Series EE savings bonds in that they don't offer periodic interest payments, or "coupons." Instead, they sell at a deep discount to their face value. That way, investors are reasonably guaranteed a certain rate of return over a long period of time without having to worry about reinvesting their income.

For example, a zero coupon bond with a face value of $1000 and a maturity date 15 years from now may sell for $313. In this arrangement, an investor will be earning about 8 percent a year. The downside of the arrangement is that the investor is required to pay taxes on the gains that accrue each year, even though they have not yet been paid. Because of the tax consequences, these bonds may be best suited for some sort of tax-sheltered account, like an IRA.

Inflation Protected Bonds

Other more recently issued U.S. government securities are Treasury Inflation Protected Securities, or TIPS, and the Series I savings bond, commonly known as the I Bond. Both of these investments address that basic enemy of investing known as inflation. While most other types of investments are purchased for their ability to rise more rapidly than inflation, TIPS and I Bonds are *guaranteed* to do so. This is because their rates of return are directly tied to a common measure of inflation—the CPI-U, or Consumer Price Index for All Urban Consumers.

Twice a year each security is readjusted to better reflect a return greater than the current rate of inflation. The yield for I Bonds is adjusted every six months. With TIPS, it's the principal, rather than the yield, that is adjusted, and that takes place every six months as well. What this means is that investors who purchase TIPS must pay federal taxes on returns even though they don't get the additions to the principal until the bond is redeemed. As such, TIPS are also much better suited for retirement accounts or other tax-sheltered situations.

The rate on the I Bond is composed of a fixed rate plus another annualized inflation rate based on the CPI-U. A complicated formula is applied to the two rates to come up with the final rate. The rates are set on the first day of every November and every May. The beauty of I Bonds is that they're risk-free, exempt from state and local taxes, adjusted for inflation semiannually, and free from federal taxation until they're redeemed. Under certain circumstances, returns on the bonds are free from federal tax if they're used to pay college tuition and fees. They can be held for up to 30 years before redemption. On the flip side, they can't be redeemed until you've held them for at least six months, and there's a penalty of three months earnings if you redeem them before five years from the date of purchase. In other words, a bond cashed in after 18 months would only pay 15 months of earnings.

I Bonds are bought at face value, without a sales charge, through banks, not brokers. Potential investors should be aware that they'll be responsible for keeping the bonds safe until redemption. Treat bonds like real money, because without the paper certificates, you'll have a hard time proving that you made the investment. Series I bonds are available in denominations ranging from $50 to $10,000, and there's a limit of $30,000 per investor (meaning Social Security number) per calendar year.

TIPS are offered by government auction, and are commonly available in 10- and 30-year denominations. The five-year variety has been phased out. The principal amount on TIPS is adjusted for inflation, measured by the CPI-U, twice a year. Semiannual interest payments reflect these adjustments. As previously mentioned, TIPS are better suited to retirement accounts, especially since inflation protection is an important consideration for a long-term time frame. And although inflation has been tame since the early 1990s, it's unlikely that it will stay entirely contained forever. Even if *deflation* occurs, you won't lose money.

Municipal Bonds

Municipal bonds are also issued by governments. Towns, cities, and local agencies all issue "muni" bonds as a way to borrow money for projects.

These bonds are particularly attractive to wealthy individuals because they come with even better tax privileges than federally issued bonds. Their interest income is almost always exempt from both federal taxes and those, if any, of the state and locality where the bond was issued. However, any capital gains are still subject to regular tax rates.

The minimum principal amount of municipal bonds tends to be high, usually around $5000 or more. In addition, it's possible for a municipality to find itself in financial trouble (more on this in the next chapter). This makes municipal bonds riskier than other government-issued securities. Still, the tax exemption these bonds offer can make them very attractive to investors. It also helps municipalities get loans at lower rates, since the tax advantages make up for lower yields.

Just how much of a difference do these tax breaks make? For an investor in a hypothetical 30 percent tax bracket, a 4 percent tax-free bond is the same as a 5.7 percent taxable yield. Of course, for comparisons like these to make sense, you should be comparing bonds with similar yields and credit ratings. For an even better idea of the advantage tax-free investments can afford, check out Table 8-1:

TABLE 8-1. **Tax-Exempt vs. Taxable Yields**

	Coupon Yield on Tax-exempt Bond				
	2.00%	3.00%	4.00%	5.00%	6.00%
Federal Income Tax Rate	Equivalent Yield of a Taxable Bond				
10.00%	2.22%	3.33%	4.44%	5.56%	6.67%
27.00%	2.74%	4.11%	5.48%	6.85%	8.22%
30.00%	2.86%	4.29%	5.71%	7.14%	8.57%
35.00%	3.08%	4.62%	6.15%	7.69%	9.23%
38.60%	3.26%	4.89%	6.51%	8.14%	9.77%

As you can see, for investors in high tax brackets, investments like muni bonds can make a lot of sense. It's often been said, "You only need to get rich once." As such, many wealthy investors choose to let their good fortunes work for them, without taking on unnecessary risk or tax burdens.

Corporate Bonds

Earlier, we noted that corporations issue stock in order to raise money for their businesses. Bonds offer companies another way to raise capital. Like their government counterparts, companies allow investors to purchase bonds, usually with the promise of favorable interest payments for the life of the loan. And like government bonds, corporate bonds come in many different flavors.

Callable Bonds

Many corporate bonds are **callable**, which means that the issuer has the right to retire the bond before its actual maturity date; that is, during predetermined times, the borrower can pay back the loan at a preset price, usually one representing a small premium to the original amount borrowed. Keep in mind, the right to do so is solely up to the issuer of the bond; the bondholder has no say in the matter. Most federal bonds do not have this feature, although many municipal bonds do.

The ability to call back a bond before its term ends is especially beneficial to the issuer because it provides the opportunity to refinance a loan if interest rates drop sharply. For example, say Company ABC issues a 20-year corporate bond at a rate of 8.5 percent interest, with a provision that it can be called away from holders after five years for a price of $104 for every $100 in principal. If, five years later, interest rates for similar bonds have come down to 5 percent, the issuer would probably call back the original bonds and issue new bonds at the lower rate.

If you're considering investing in a bond with a callable feature, there's something you need to be aware of. The feature allows you to get hurt by *both* rising and falling interest rates. This is because in addition to the adverse effect that rate increases have on almost all bonds, the call provision will likely be exercised if interest rates go lower, which will also hurt you.

In fact, anytime interest rates decline by 2 or 3 percentage points, a callable bond will likely get bought back by its issuer. What's worse, if that happens, an investor will probably have a hard time finding a similar payout from another investment of equal quality. So before you invest in a bond, be sure to check out whether it has a callable feature. If it does, carefully read over the terms of the agreement. And always keep in mind that, by nature, the cash flow from callable bonds is somewhat unpredictable.

Convertible Bonds

Another common type of corporate bond, the **convertible bond,** can be converted into a company's stock. This option provides one more way of fighting inflation. Convertible bonds typically have many of the safeguards that regular bonds afford, with an added feature that lets an investor trade in the bond for a specific number of shares of the issuer's common stock. The main benefit of this feature is that if a company's stock price rises, so does the value of the bond.

However, this advantage comes at a price—usually lower interest payments than comparable nonconvertible bonds. Still, for investors looking for income and the upside potential of stocks, convertible bonds may be a good choice.

Private Placements

One last type of bond, one that you'll probably never see, is a **private placement**. These are privately negotiated loans that aren't offered to the public. For example, a company may borrow money from an institution or an individual at terms that are different from those available in the public debt market. Of course, even if you're wealthy enough to participate in this sort of arrangement, there's a disadvantage—little liquidity. In the end, it's just as easy to find worthwhile bonds from the categories above.

Summary

There are two main types of bonds: those issued by governments and those issued by corporations. In both cases, bondholders are essentially loaning money to the bond issuer at a predetermined interest rate. Bonds issued by the federal government are among the safest investments around; other bonds carry great risk. To learn more about determining a bond's risk, read on.

CHAPTER 9

Researching Bonds

If you plan on investing in individual bonds, you will potentially be researching the two main types of bonds: corporate and government. Government bonds range the gamut—everything from ultrasafe, U.S. Treasury-issued savings bonds to bonds issued by municipalities, aptly nicknamed "muni bonds." Corporate bonds, on the other hand, all come from companies.

Historically, corporate bonds have been considered safer than their stock counterparts. This is because a bondholder is a creditor of a company, while a stockholder is a partial owner of a company. As a partial owner, a stockholder can only lay claim to a proportionate amount of the remaining assets and earnings *after* all the creditors get their crack at the place. In other words, if a business goes bust, a bondholder is more likely to get something at the end of the proceedings.

But don't get the wrong idea—bonds aren't necessarily safe. This has been especially true over the last few decades, as wide swings in interest rates and a deluge of lower quality corporate bonds, known as "junk bonds," have affected the market. Even many government bonds, especially municipals, can be quite risky. Don't believe it? What would-be investors fail to realize is that even well-known cities and counties have filed for bankruptcy in the past. A good example is the bankruptcy of wealthy Orange County, California, in 1994. Even New York City came very close to declaring the dreaded B word back in the mid-1970s.

HOW DOES A WEALTHY COUNTY GO BANKRUPT?

Orange County, which sits just outside Los Angeles and contains many of California's most famous beach towns, has traditionally been considered one of the wealthiest areas in the United States. How is it, then, that the county was forced to declare bankruptcy in December 1994?

The answer in this case proves an especially important point—the county went bankrupt because of overly risky investing practices. The county treasurer at the time, Bob Citron, had been delivering stellar investment results for a number of years. His track record was so great that he had to turn away money from outside entities looking to get in on the action. Meanwhile, some local municipalities were issuing additional public investments so they could get more money into the nearly $8 billion of county money already in the pool.

What they didn't know was that Citron had been getting his results through a number of risky measures. For starters, he had essentially opened a margin account, by borrowing additional funds on the county's money. In fact, the portfolio was leveraged for 200 percent of its value, meaning that Citron was investing three times the money he actually had. In addition, he was investing this borrowed money in derivatives, which are leveraged investments on their own.

For a while, Citron's strategy of betting that interest rates would continue to fall worked. However, a series of subsequent interest rate hikes cost the fund well over a billion dollars in losses, sending financial shockwaves throughout Orange County. The portfolio was liquidated, Citron resigned, and Orange County was bankrupt. Citron later plead guilty to six felony counts.

Credit Ratings

So, how do you know how safe a bond really is? While the absolute answer is that you never know for sure, there are ratings systems that help investors assess the creditworthiness of a particular bond issuer. These ratings are produced by a number of agencies. The two largest and most influential are Moody's and Standard & Poor's, both of which rate bonds on alphabetical scales, although each uses the letters slightly differently. Table 9-1 compares the two systems.

TABLE 9-1. Comparable Ratings from S&P and Moody's

Standard & Poor's *	Moody's #	
AAA	Aaa	Highest quality
AA	Aa	High quality
A	A	Upper medium quality
BBB	Baa	Medium grade
BB	Ba	Somewhat speculative
B	B	Low grade, speculative
CCC	Caa	Low grade, default possible
CC	Ca	Low grade, partial recovery possible
C	C	Default, recovery unlikely
D		Bond is in default

* A + or – may be added to any S&P rating to signify relative strength or weakness within that given rating.

A 1, 2, or 3 numerical modifier may be placed after any Moody's rating to signify that the company is in the higher end of its group (1), the middle range of its group (2), or at the lower end of its group (3).

For a bondholder, the major question is: "What are the odds that the borrower will pay me back?" By constantly staying on top of a borrower's financial situation, rating agencies help answer this question. Although the ratings aren't equal to investment recommendations, many borrowers and lenders treat them as such.

In most cases, when one or more of the major ratings agencies downgrades a borrower's rating, the borrower will have a harder time getting more financing. This ultimately leads to the borrower having to pay higher interest rates on money borrowed. Thus, the relationship can be thought of as: The likelier you are to pay back the bondholder, the less additional money you'll have to pay out over the life of the loan. Makes sense, doesn't it?

By the way, in some extreme cases the process can turn into a vicious cycle. In other words, for some companies, a rating downgrade and an ensuing inability to borrow more money may lead to an even weaker business and further credit downgrades. As such, investors should take credit ratings seriously, even those who are holding stocks instead of bonds.

The interest rate on U.S. government securities is sometimes called the "risk-free rate of return" because there's no chance that the federal treasury will default on its obligations. This is because the government can always issue more money—"run the printing press"—to wipe out its debt. This, however, leads to inflation rather than deflation.

On the other hand, the risk on corporate bonds varies greatly, with almost all of them having a greater chance of default than those from the federal government. That's why they typically pay higher interest rates when they borrow.

Ditto for municipal borrowers. Standard & Poor's assigns credit ratings to both of the riskier bond categories. As you can see from Table 9-1, AAA is the highest rating a bond can carry. The rating indicates that a borrower possesses all the resources it needs to pay back both principal and interest. As you get further down the list, the prospects of getting a return on your money get murkier. Still, any bond with a rating above BBB is known as *investment grade*.

Once you get below investment grade, you find yourself in the universe of the aforementioned junk bond (often you'll see a euphemism like "high-yield" instead). Corporate junk bonds generally pay much higher yields than their investment grade counterparts.

Of course, there's a stronger chance that they'll never pay back their bondholders. A Standard & Poor's study of more than 7300 bonds it rated since 1981 found that just 2.1 percent of investment-grade corporate bonds defaulted within 15 years of their issuance, with even lower rates for high-quality muni bonds. In contrast, 23 percent of junk bonds had defaulted within 15 years.

Junk bonds became popular in the 1980s, when corporate takeovers were all the rage. Perhaps the most famous character associated with these investments is Michael Milken, known as "the junk bond king." While at the helm of Drexel Burnham Lambert Inc., Milken used the assets to facilitate a number of corporate takeovers. In fact, Gordon Gekko, the main character of the 1987 movie *Wall Street*, was largely based on Milken. Both Milken and another junk bond junkie, Ivan Boesky, spent time in prison due to their dubious investment practices, and to this day junk bonds carry a particular stigma.

The fact that junk bonds have non-investment-grade credit ratings also precludes many professional money managers from owning them. However, this doesn't mean that investing in junk bonds can't be profitable. Some have provided investors with regular streams of interest and have risen in price.

An interesting side note is that, historically, junk bonds have done extremely well in the early stages of an economic recovery. In the 12 months after recessions dating from 2002 back to 1949, high-yield corporate bonds returned an average of 14.2 percent, versus 2.5 percent for long-term government securities, according to calculations by T. Rowe Price, an investment management firm. As always, your particular goals and risk tolerance should help you decide whether a particular investment is right for your portfolio.

Other Factors Affecting Bond Prices

More than just the creditworthiness of the issuer affects a bond's price. Returns available from alternative investments, the rate of inflation, and the timeline for interest payments and return of principal are also significant factors.

As a general rule, the longer the time to **maturity**—the date on which the borrower must pay back the money—the more volatile a bond's price is likely to be. In addition, longer-term bonds usually must provide higher interest rates since investors are committing money for longer periods of time, which carries along with it a greater level of risk.

For the most part, a bond's interest rate reflects an assumed level of inflation plus a premium for the type of risk a lender is taking. Unlike cash dividends from stocks, interest payments from bonds typically remain fixed over a bond's life span. However, as we noted while discussing inflation, it's unlikely that a given amount of money will have the same buying power as it did a few years before. That's why investors require a higher yield for longer-term securities. Typically, bond prices react favorably to periods of low expected inflation. Likewise, their prices tend to decline when investors expect higher inflation.

An attractive feature of bonds, especially higher quality issues, is the relatively predictable flow of interest and principal payments. The sensitivity of bond prices to changes in the general interest rate environment presents an element of risk for bond traders, though. During times of higher interest rates, bond prices tend to go down. This is because newer bond issues are likely to present higher yields than those that were previously issued. Therefore, the older bonds are less attractive than the newer ones. Conversely, bond prices tend to go up as interest rates go down, since the older, higher-yielding bonds are more attractive investments.

Reinvestment Rate Risk

If a bond is held to maturity, interim changes in interest rates and bond prices are likely to be of less concern than if a bond is sold prematurely. However, **reinvestment rate risk**, which is also affected by interest rates and changes in bond prices, is still a consideration. Reinvestment rate risk is the chance that future bond investments may not yield as much as current ones. Thus, even bond investors who keep their bonds until maturity will face reinvestment risk at some point. Here's an example:

Taylor is receiving a 9 percent annual yield ($90 on a $1000 bond). During that time, the interest rate environment changes to the point where a new buyer of the same type of bond is only receiving a 7.5 percent yield. The problem for Taylor is that he'll now have a harder time earning interest on the interest that his current bond is providing. To earn the same rate of return, he'll have to take on additional risk. Of course, things can also work the other way—the interest rate environment could lead to more favorable bond yields, which would provide Taylor with even greater returns on his future investments (although this would also cause the value of his bonds to go down).

While the concept might sound strange at first, especially since investments are almost always somewhat uncertain, reinvestment rate risk is a valid concern for bond investors, especially those looking to bonds for a stable stream of income and appreciation as part of a larger, long-term portfolio. In other words, it makes it difficult for an investor to make any long-term assumptions about how much the bond portion of a portfolio will earn. This is primarily because uncertain future yields lead to uncertain rates of compounding interest.

So, what can be done to limit reinvestment rate risk?

The truth is that no amount of research can ease the problem of reinvestment rate risk. However, a good strategy can certainly help smooth things over. Many investors cope with reinvestment rate risk by establishing a rolling bond portfolio. Such a portfolio includes bonds with varying maturity dates, also known as having "laddered maturities." For example, an investor with $100,000 slated for bonds could purchase 10 $10,000 bonds with maturities spaced two years apart, ranging from two years to 20 years.

Just as other forms of diversification help mitigate risk, staggering the dates of the bonds in your portfolio ensures that not all of your portfolio will have to be reinvested at a time when conditions are unfavorable. It also helps you achieve a blended yield of both shorter-term and longer-term returns. Lastly, setting up a bond portfolio in this way provides better liquidity since a portion of the overall investment will automatically convert to cash periodically (every two years in the example above).

Summary

As creditors, bond investors should be most concerned about whether their loan (and the associated interest payments) will be repaid. To that end, you should pay close attention to a company's credit rating throughout your tenure as an investor. In addition, you should also pay close attention to interest rates, since bond prices move in the opposite direction. And while it's entirely possible to research and maintain a portfolio of bond investments, for many people a bond mutual fund might provide the easiest and safest way to participate in this tricky investment class. For more on mutual funds, continue on to the next chapter.

PART 4

Funds

CHAPTER 10

What Are Funds?

After reading about stocks, bonds, and other forms of investments, you might by now assume that managing your investments can become a full-time job. You might have also realized that to get the kind of diversification recommended will take a good deal of money. The truth is, most investors feel this way. Fortunately, there are investments that lessen both of these concerns—funds. Essentially, funds are pooled investments run by one or more professional money managers according to a predetermined strategy.

Mutual Funds

Mutual funds are the most common type of fund investment for individual investors. All mutual funds are required to hold to a particular type of defined strategy, which is outlined in the fund's prospectus. For many funds, the strategy is very specific; for others, it is less so. One thing to note is that any mutual fund, no matter what its stated strategy, is permitted to invest 20 percent of its assets in holdings that fall outside the boundaries of its strategy.

Through mutual funds, investors can make generalized investment decisions without spending lots of time worrying about the day-to-day research and decision-making processes of running a diversified portfolio. There are a number of different ways to classify mutual funds—from the way they're managed to the types of investments they purchase.

The first thing you should know about mutual funds is that they don't come for free. As in other aspects of life, people who work for you expect to get paid. There are a few different ways for the people behind funds to get their compensation. Some may use only one way, while others might use a combination of ways. Perhaps the most common route is through a management fee. The name says it all—this is an annual fee charged to investors for the money managers' services. The structure of funds' management fees varies, so it's best to look closely at this area before investing in a particular fund.

A lot of mutual funds can also have what are known as 12b-1 plans, which allow funds to reduce their assets under management by 0.25 to 1.25 percent annually to cover their marketing and distribution expenses. In other words, funds with 12b-1 plans can use your money to woo new investors to their products. If you can find suitable investments without these plans, you'd probably be much better off.

Also, since many funds are sold by third parties—brokers and such—many also charge **loads**, or sales fees. These fees are given back to the person who sold the fund to you. Those funds that don't charge sales fees are known as **no-load** funds. They are typically available directly from the companies that run them. There are two types of loads: up-front loads and back-end loads, or redemption fees. When looking at potential funds, you should be aware of how loads can affect your returns, and especially whether the fund's performance will offset the fees over time. A fund that charges a load will have to post better gains than a no-load fund. Consider this example:

Craig has $5000 to invest. His two main fund choices vary in their fee structures. The first is a no-load fund, while the second charges an 8 percent front load. Because of the second fund's load, Craig would only be investing $4600: 8 percent of $5,000 = $400, and $5000 − $400 leaves $4600. What this means is that over five years, the second fund would have to advance about 11.9 percent annually (before taxes) just to match a 10 percent return from the no-load fund. Table 10-1 shows the progress of each investment throughout the five years.

TABLE 10-1. Effect of an 8% Load on a $5,000 Investment

Start	$4600	$5000
Compounding at:	11.90%	10%
Year 1	$5147	$5500
Year 2	5760	6050
Year 3	6445	6655
Year 4	7212	7321
Year 5	8071	8053

Keep in mind, the longer you plan to hold a fund, the less impact a load will have on your returns. However, the advantage of investing in no-load funds is pretty clear.

Two Ways of Classifying Funds

Beyond their fee structures, there are a few other common ways to break down the various types of mutual funds. Here are two ways of classifying funds, as well as the most popular types of mutual funds available to investors:

ACTIVELY VS. PASSIVELY MANAGED FUNDS

All mutual funds are run by professional investors. In most cases, these fund managers make individual investment decisions within the context of their defined strategy. The object of these decisions is to outperform the returns of some corresponding benchmark. In most cases, the benchmark is an index.

A fund manager committed to buying large-cap stocks might try to outperform the S&P 500. To do this, she can choose which individual stocks to buy, as long as they fall into the larger category of growth stocks. In addition, the manager can choose to allocate the funds under her management in any way that she chooses. Her portfolio might consist of 10 percent of one stock and 5 percent of 18 others. The decisions are solely hers. These mutual funds are known as actively managed funds since their managers make independent decisions in an effort to outperform some broad measure of their particular market.

However, some mutual funds do just the opposite. In an effort to *match* the performance of a particular market, they try to replicate the performance of a benchmark. A mutual fund wishing to match the returns of the stock market might just purchase the 500 companies that make up the S&P 500 index (in the same proportions as the actual index). Whenever a change in the index takes place, the mangers make the exact same change in their portfolio. In this way, they're completely removed from the decision-making process. Thus, funds run in this manner are called passively managed funds.

In fact, there are funds that do follow the S&P 500 to the letter. Other funds mimic the returns of other indexes. Many experts recommend passive funds, especially index funds, as a sound way to participate in the stock market. This is because they offer investors a clearly defined strategy and exposure to a particular investment class, as well as solid diversification. In addition, it's likely that passively managed funds will be less expensive to purchase than their actively managed brethren. This is because the cost of marketing and running such funds is cheaper, and some of the savings are passed on to investors.

OPEN-END VS. CLOSED-END FUNDS

Another way to differentiate between mutual funds is through the way investors are able to participate in them. The two major categories are open-end funds and closed-end funds.

Open-end funds are by far the more popular category. Funds of this type continuously accept new money, and thus issue additional shares. It also means that they're always putting this new money to work in the financial markets. When an investor wishes to cash out of the fund, his shares will generally be bought back by the fund for the value of all the underlying investments that the shares represent. This number is known as the **net asset value**, or NAV. The mathematical expression of the NAV is the current value of the securities and cash that the fund has, divided by the number of shares it has outstanding. Table 10-2 provides an example of a NAV calculation.

TABLE 10-2. Calculating a Stock Fund's NAV

Cash and Equivalent Holdings	$300,000
Add Today's Total Market Value of Stocks Owned	5,000,000
Total Assets	$5,300,000
Subtract Current Liabilities (includes expenses)	100,000
Total Net Assets	$5,200,000
Divide by number of fund shares currently outstanding	100,000
Net Asset Value (NAV) per share	$5.20

Closed-end funds, as the name suggests, are not open to new investment dollars. Instead, these funds issue a set number of shares during inception. Investors who want to participate after the initial offering must buy the shares on the secondary market, much like regular stocks. In fact, a variety of closed-end funds are traded on the NYSE. Although shares of a closed-end fund can trade above their NAV, many more actually trade at a discount to this figure. Why? Largely because a fund may have unrealized capital gains on its investments, and the discount reflects the potential tax liability that a new investor faces.

Also, there may be liquidity concerns with certain funds. In this case, investors are only willing to purchase a fund at a discount to its NAV because they believe that the fund might have a hard time actually selling its investments at the prices they're currently fetching.

For example, if a fund has a large stake in a particular stock, it's unlikely that it would be able to unload all of that stock at the current market price. That's because the very nature of a large sale— that is, a big supply—would inherently lower the demand, and thus the stock's price. Funds that invest in junk bonds are especially prone to liquidity concerns.

Common Types of Mutual Funds

Most mutual funds invest in stocks, bonds, or a combination of both. We'll go into this by category and subcategory. Table 10-3 summarizes the long-term characteristics of both common types of mutual funds.

TABLE 10-3. Long-Term Characteristics of Mutual Funds

	Capital Gains	Income	Total Return	Risk Level
Stock Funds				
Aggressive Growth	Very High	Low	Very High	Very High
Growth	High	Low	High	High
Income	Low	High	Moderate	Moderate
Growth/Income	Moderate	Moderate	Moderate	Moderate
Industry Specific	Varies	Varies	Varies	Varies
Precious Metals	High	Low	Varies	High
Global	High	Moderate	High	High
International	Very High	Low	High	High
Bond Funds				
High-grade Corporate	Low	High	Moderate	Low
High-yield Corporate	Very High	High	High	Very High
U.S. Government	Low	Moderate	Moderate	Low
Municipal Bonds	Low	Moderate	Low	Low

STOCK FUNDS

As the name implies, stock funds are made up of a portfolio of stock investments. There are many different ways to categorize the myriad stock funds available to investors:

GROWTH VS. VALUE FUNDS. Many funds will classify themselves as either growth or value funds. Growth funds will likely contain stocks that are poised for superior price appreciation over the near term. In general, they will be better suited for aggressive investors looking for big gains. On the other hand, value funds usually stick to stocks that look like bargains based on one or more fundamental measures. Value managers will often hold their positions for long periods because they recognize that it often takes a long time for other people to recognize the attractiveness of a stock they believe in.

The late 1990s perfectly frames the perils of both growth and value fund managers. During the period of great enthusiasm for technology stocks, which fell almost exclusively into the growth category, many value fund managers could only sit on the sidelines, with performance numbers that looked pale in comparison to the impressive gains being racked up by their counterparts. However, as those same technology shares came tumbling back to realistic valuations, and investors fled toward more traditional stocks, many value fund managers found themselves in the limelight once again.

The lesson is that either camp can do well depending on the current environment. Thus, investors might be wise to make sure they have exposure to both categories. To that end, there are also stock funds that wouldn't claim allegiance to either growth or value stocks, opting instead to buy whatever issues they find attractive at the time.

OTHER STOCK FUND CLASSIFICATIONS. Stock funds might also be categorized by the size or the type of companies they invest in. There are funds that invest solely in smaller companies and those that stick only to the largest ones. There are other funds that invest in mainly technology stocks. Focusing on a particular type of company is advantageous to the fund manager since many of these areas require specific knowledge.

For example, to successfully invest in biotechnology stocks, it would be helpful to have a strong background in science, either personally or through a research team. Likewise, smaller-cap companies are often valued differently than their larger-cap brethren. By running a fund that specializes in small caps, a manager will likely be better in tune with assessing these investments. Investors also benefit from funds with specific focuses because they provide straightforward exposure to specific types of investments. Through them, investors are better able to construct well-diversified portfolios.

One word of caution, though: just because a fund claims that it's focused on a particular type of stock doesn't mean that 100 percent of its assets are invested there. As we said earlier, mutual funds do have some leeway in their allocations. If possible, do an occasional check on your fund's holdings just to make sure that your money is invested where you want it. Investors are sometimes surprised to find out that their technology stock fund is invested in a number of the same names as their large-cap stock fund.

INTERNATIONAL STOCK FUNDS. There are also funds that specialize in seeking gains abroad, by investing in international companies, whether globally or with a focus on a specific region. These funds help investors overcome the additional challenges of foreign investing, which include higher commissions when purchasing foreign stocks directly, lack of information, and foreign taxation of any dividends received. Foreign funds also benefit from the specialized knowledge necessary for investing in a tricky area, which we discussed above.

GOLD FUNDS. Some investors turn to this type of stock mutual fund, especially during tougher times. Truth be told, gold isn't quite the investment it once was. There are a number of reasons for this, including the fact that most currencies are no longer backed by the metal. However, to some people gold continues to offer one of the few safe havens from inflation.

While many so-called "gold bugs" argue that there's no security like having a few gold bars stashed away under the mattress, other investors wish to participate in any hint of a gold rush without all the weight in their pockets and find gold funds a nice alternative. Most gold funds invest in the stocks of mining companies. By doing so, they hope to indirectly profit from any increase in the price of gold.

Gold, gold stocks, and gold funds, tend to do best during inflationary times or during weak stock markets. Although the precious metals markets can be volatile, some investors look toward these funds as an additional way to diversify their portfolios.

BOND FUNDS

From our earlier discussion of bonds, you probably got the idea that investing in most types of bonds is difficult for individual investors. If you did, you're right. Many types of individual bonds are difficult to purchase, and all of the variables involved mean a lot of time researching, time you may not have. Fortunately, like stock funds, there are many types of bond funds available to investors. In fact, you're probably better off getting some bond exposure through bond funds rather than through individual bonds.

Bond funds offer a level of diversification that would be unobtainable for most of us. In addition, like their stock counterparts, bond fund managers are well versed on the specific factors that affect bond prices and yields.

There are many types of bond funds, running the gamut from very safe ones that invest in Treasuries to those that specialize in highly speculative junk bonds. You may choose to purchase one general bond fund for the fixed-income portion of your portfolio, or you may opt to invest in a few specific types of funds, depending on your individual goals. However, as with any fund, be sure to consider all the costs involved, as well as the fund's long-term performance. Like stocks, bonds are subject to periods of strength and weakness. Looking at a bond fund's performance over a relatively short period of time may not give you a good idea of how well it will do over a longer period.

BALANCED FUNDS

For investors looking for absolute diversification, or for a more conservative approach, there are funds that invest in both stocks and bonds. They're known as balanced funds, but don't let the name fool you—these funds aren't necessarily invested in 50 percent of each asset class. Balanced funds lend themselves nicely to places like 401(k) plans, since they're pretty much a stand-alone diversified portfolio. While they might not offer the same level of appreciation as an all-stock fund, they're probably a bit safer, and their returns should be more level over time.

Other Types of Funds

In addition to mutual funds, there are other kinds of funds available to investors. Some were designed for investors seeking diversification without the high costs associated with many mutual funds. Others are like private mutual funds for wealthy people.

Exchange Traded Funds

Exchange Traded Funds (ETFs) are a growing category of investments that act like mutual funds but trade like individual stocks. For that reason, they're akin to closed-end funds; however, they're composed of a set basket of stocks, much like a passively managed fund. Thus, with ETFs investors get the best of both worlds—an easily traded investment with a set level of diversity.

ETFs were designed as another way for investors to match the performance of an index or a particular group of stocks, including those in a chosen sector or region. For example, investors can purchase Standard & Poor's Depository Receipts, known as SPDRs or "Spiders," as an alternative to investing in a mutual fund tracking the "500." Like index funds, SPDRs represent ownership of the 500 underlying companies in the S&P 500 index.

The advantages of ETFs are many. Because they trade on a regular stock exchange, they're relatively liquid. Some ETFs, like the Nasdaq 100 Trust (commonly known by its ticker symbol, QQQ or "cubes"), trade millions of shares a day— about 70 million shares, in fact. ETFs also offer investors much of the same diversity as other types of funds. And although every buy or sell will involve some commission cost, the overall expense of investing in ETFs will be much lower than a mutual fund equivalent, assuming you trade them through a discount broker.

Of course, you'll still need to carefully study what particular basket of stocks you're purchasing, especially if you plan on buying more than one ETF. As with funds, it's possible for more than one ETF to contain the same stock, or stocks, thus giving you a false sense of diversification.

Hedge Funds

If you spend any amount of time listening to stock market commentators, you'll certainly hear some talk about hedge funds. No, these aren't for investors wishing to invest in lawn service companies. However, it does take a lot of green to get into a hedge fund.

Hedge funds are private investment funds for wealthy individuals and institutional investors. By law, you must have an annual income exceeding $250,000 and investable assets of around $1 million to participate in the world of hedge funds. This is mainly because hedge funds are limited partnerships that operate like unregulated mutual funds. As such, they carry substantial risk.

These pools of money are run by professional investors, but the difference is, they don't have to adhere to particular strategies. Some hedge fund investors may not even know where their money is invested at all. Still, most expect outsized gains in the end. Hedge funds, by nature, are speculative operations. The name comes from the fact that many hedge funds look to take advantage of both up and down markets by buying and shorting stocks. In addition, many hedge funds invest in other areas like bonds and options. They may also look to participate in currency markets.

Although many hedge funds do have defined, sensible strategies, it's not uncommon for a hedge fund manager to place a huge bet on one particular idea. For that reason, hedge fund investors need both deep pockets and strong stomachs. A good example is the recent collapse of Eifuku, a Japanese hedge fund. The fund, established in 2000, delivered a solid gain of 18 percent in 2001. In 2002 it skyrocketed up 76 percent, while, over the same period, the S&P 500 fell 23 percent. However, in January 2003 the fund collapsed over a period of seven days. Many of its investors were themselves Wall Street professionals, including legendary investor George Soros, widely considered one of the greatest traders of all time. Such a quick rise and fall clearly illustrates the risky nature of many hedge funds.

And hedge fund implosions can affect not only their investors, but also entire markets. In September 1998, the impending collapse of the ironically named Long-Term Capital Management hedge fund caused widespread panic throughout world stock markets. Only through a government-facilitated, Wall Street–backed bailout was tragedy narrowly averted.

Summary

Mutual funds allow investors to get the diversification they need; however, many come with substantial costs. For investors looking to participate in a broad area of the market, with high liquidity and low costs, Exchange Traded Funds provide a nice alternative. And for those people with lots of money to burn, there are plenty of hedge funds open for business.

CHAPTER 11

Researching Funds

If you decide that mutual funds have a place in your portfolio, you'd be wise to do some careful research before purchasing them. The media is quick to point out that the majority of actively managed mutual funds underperform the general stock market. And guess what? It's true.

While the numbers change from year to year, the majority of mutual fund managers consistently do worse than the S&P 500. One S&P study showed that for the five years ended September 30, 2002, the S&P 500 index and the S&P Barra Growth index outperformed 65 percent of actively managed funds. This, despite the fact that three of the five years were down market years, in which actively managed funds typically have an advantage over passive investments. For a longer picture of how mutual funds stack up to the S&P 500, check out Table 11-1.

Because most active funds underperform, and because you'll get diversification more easily, and less expensively, with index funds, you'd be wise to consider them. And as we pointed out in the last chapter, ETFs also provide cost advantages for those investors looking for more focused funds.

Still, there are also many good reasons to invest in actively managed funds, and there are just as many good actively managed funds to invest in—the key is finding them. In this chapter, we'll talk more about some basics to look at in order for you to determine whether a fund deserves your money. Even if you're planning on an index fund, read on, since some of these topics apply to them too.

[149]

TABLE 11-1. General Domestic Equity Funds that Beat S&P 500 Index

	S&P 500 Return	% That Beat Index
1987	5.10	26%
1988	16.61	46%
1989	31.69	21%
1990	–3.10	38%
1991	30.47	57%
1992	7.62	58%
1993	10.08	61%
1994	1.32	24%
1995	37.53	15%
1996	22.95	23%
1997	33.35	10%
1998	28.58	17%
1999	21.04	49%
2000	–9.10	65%
2001	–11.88	48%
2002	–22.09	43%

Note: Data from 1999 includes survivorship bias.
Domestic universe excludes balanced (or hybrid) and sector funds; includes index funds and multiple share classes.

The Prospectus

Every fund is required by law to prepare a document for prospective investors, aptly called a **prospectus**. In this document, investors can learn about a fund's investment philosophy, its management, and its financials. This last subject is covered in the "financial highlights" section, which is probably the most important part of any prospectus.

Before you put a single dollar into a fund, you should take a long, hard look at its prospectus. While much of it will contain flowery marketing language, if you know what you're looking for, you'll still be able to make an informed decision simply based on the information it provides.

Costs

The first thing you should look at when evaluating a fund is its cost structure. As we noted in the last chapter, funds don't let you in the door for free; however, the amount of money you pay in fees can vary greatly from fund to fund. More important, in the world of funds, you don't necessarily get what you pay for. In fact, high costs are one of the main reasons that many funds fail to better their benchmarks. Consider this example:

Fund A charges its shareholders 2.5 percent a year for managing their money. Fund B only charges 0.5 percent. A difference of 2 percent isn't that much, right? Wrong. After 50 years, a $10,000 investment earning 10 percent a year will be worth $1,170,000. The same amount earning 8 percent a year would be worth only $470,000.

This brings us to the first component of a fund's cost: the expense ratio.

Expense Ratio

Mutual funds need all sorts of money to continue their operations. They have to produce slick marketing brochures, fund managers have to fly all over the country kicking the tires of potential investments, and preparing all of those government filings means a lot of overtime. Of course, funds figure the best way to pay for all of these things is to pass the costs along to shareholders. Here are the most common operating fees that funds charge:

INVESTMENT ADVISORY FEE. Also known as the management fee, this is the amount of money that actually goes to the person or people managing the mutual fund. It will cost shareholders about 0.75 percent of their money every year.

ADMINISTRATIVE FEE. This includes all of those little day-to-day things like postage, record keeping, and touch-tone phone menus. Although they rarely eat up more than 0.5 percent of a fund's annual assets, the amount still varies significantly from fund to fund.

12B-1 FEE. In many ways, this fee is the biggest kick in the pants, since it covers a fund's annual marketing costs as well as any distributions it makes. So, the bad news is that anyone paying a 12b-1 fee is paying for the same glossy brochures that smarter investors are tossing in their wastebaskets. The good news is that smarter investors know there are plenty of funds that don't charge 12b-1 fees at all.

By now you're probably somewhat confused. That's precisely the point of all of these fees. Fortunately, all you really need to look at is the **expense ratio**, which is the total percentage of annual assets that a fund takes to cover all of the operational costs mentioned above.

Many funds have expense ratios in excess of 2 percent; however, you'd generally be better off looking for funds with expense ratios lower than 1 percent. Also, though most index funds offer fairly low expense ratios, many have jumped on the "buy index funds" bandwagon, with expense ratios exceeding 1 percent. Since there's relatively little difference in index fund performance, just look for the lowest expense ratio you can find. It will probably end up being around 0.2 percent.

As an example of how costs can vary even among index funds, in 2002, Vanguard, which has long been the leader in indexing, offered an S&P 500 index fund with an expense ratio of 0.18 percent. Meanwhile, the T. Rowe Price version of the same fund charged 0.35 percent. And there were other funds charging even more!

Okay, so you get the idea—buy funds with low expense ratios. But wait, there are more costs to consider . . . things like loads.

Loads

As you may recall from the last chapter, certain mutual funds have loads and other funds are considered no-load. While the expenses we just covered above are all operational costs—or those that are claimed as operational costs—loads are just big, ugly sales commissions tacked onto funds.

FRONT LOAD

The simplest load to spot and understand is the **front load**, which is a good old American upfront sales charge. With a front load, you pay up the day you buy into a fund—maybe something like 6 percent. Unless you just say no, which is advisable.

BACK-END LOAD

Of course, funds got wise to the ease with which a front load can be spotted and rejected, so they devised a better way of charging you— the **back-end load**, sometimes camouflaged as the contingent deferred sales load (CDSL), or as "class B" shares. Would it be unfair to characterize the back-end load as simply a way to trick investors into thinking they aren't being charged a load? You be the judge. Basically, a back-end load works something like this:

If you leave the fund within the first year, you get charged 5 percent.

If you leave the fund within the second year, you get charged 4 percent.

It continues on that way, with the sales charge being reduced by 1 percent a year until the sixth. Then, if you leave, you don't get charged a fee at all.

So far it sounds like long-term investors should be okay with back-end loads, right? Well, the other part of the equation is that for every year you own a fund with a back-end load, you're also probably going to be paying a fairly hefty 12b-1 fee. So, even if you hold the fund for the five years, you're still paying a lot more than you should. Besides, why lock yourself into holding a fund for five years? What if the fund underperforms for a few years in a row? Should you have to pay the fund company just to get out of their fund? Probably not.

LEVEL LOAD

The last type of load is known as the **level load**, and sometimes as "class C" shares. With the level load, you don't have to pay anything for buying or selling the fund, except maybe a 1 percent redemption fee. However, you still get hit with a rather high 12b-1 fee. And as we've already noted, an additional 1 percent a year makes a difference.

In the end, figuring out a fund's costs can be a daunting task. Especially since the whole thing is purposely designed to be confusing. Fortunately, every fund must provide potential investors with a prospectus, as we mentioned above, and within it you'll find a fee table. Pay close attention to it, since a thorough reading will tell you exactly what your fund is asking you to pay.

Regardless of where the line between 12b-1 fee and load is drawn, in most cases your best approach is to flat out reject any fund that charges either. The only reason you might consider buying a fund with higher-than-average fees is if it's had a long history of above-average returns. Of course, even if you find a fund with reasonable fees, you'll still want to look into its history.

Fund History

The financial highlights section of a fund's prospectus will show you how well the fund has done over the past 10 years—or since its inception, if it's been around less than 10 years. You should concern yourself with the fund's total return, or capital appreciation plus dividend payments, since that's the best picture of what it has actually delivered.

Of course, when it comes to a fund's performance numbers, it's not only important that they're above average, but that they've been that way over the course of many years. There are a million funds out there touting tremendous performance numbers ("The Gainus Maximus Fund was up 350 percent last year!"), but very few of those funds have racked up solid gains for many years in a row. In some cases, a fund can be temporarily riding high from its focus.

For example, we noted earlier that many Internet funds experienced uncanny gains in the late 1990s as technology stocks soared. Likewise, most of that performance was wiped away once the technology tide turned red. The lesson here is that a slow and steady fund, one with 5 or 10 years of above-average gains, is the one you want to invest in. Thus, you should take some time to look at a fund's long-term performance numbers.

Be advised, however, that even long-term performance numbers might not tell the full story. In fact, they're just the beginning. There's no surefire way to know that a strong performance will continue, and there are other things to look at that will help you make a more informed decision—namely, the things going on behind the scenes during the fund's life span. Let's say fund A has outperformed the S&P 500 for the last seven years in a row. It sounds like a pretty attractive fund, right? But what if the fund manager responsible for all of those great years was recently replaced? You wouldn't be as ready to count on another seven years of outperformance, would you? Justifiably not. In fact, a fund's management should be considered a crucial underpinning of its performance record.

Management

It's a fairly obvious concern, but many investors fail to consider who's in charge of their money. There are a few aspects of a fund's management you'll want to look at.

Team Approach or Dictatorship?

First, you'll want to establish who's managing the fund. In some cases, an individual fund manager will be responsible for making all the major decisions. Other times, the fund will be run by a team of two or more managers. There are pros and cons to either approach; one is not necessarily better than the other. What's important is that you find out who will be making the decisions. Once you know that, you can look into whether they're worthy of managing your money. One good gauge of their ability is past experience.

Experience

Experience is a key element to successfully running money. You'll want to know how many years of experience a fund manager has. You'll also want to know how many years he's been at the fund you're currently considering. In most cases, the longer the better, since underperforming fund managers aren't usually kept around until they're ready to retire. Moreover, the longer the fund manager has been with a fund, the better his specialized knowledge probably is.

This brings up an interesting point. For funds that invest in very specific areas, it's often good to have a fund manager with a background that involves not only investing in the businesses, but also in working in the field. For example, managers of health-care funds often have scientific backgrounds.

No matter what a fund manager's current record, you'll also want to find out what other funds, if any, he's been involved with. The types of funds they were and how they performed will provide further insight into a given manager's ability and focus. A fund manager who has successfully run three different small-cap funds in 10 years, for instance, is probably a better candidate than a fund manager with 20 years of experience managing 15 different types of funds (especially if each of them seems to coincide with whatever strategy was in fashion at the time).

A fund prospectus should contain a biography of each manager involved with the fund. Since the information provided will probably be edited to cast the best possible light, you might consider using the biography as a starting point for further investigation.

One other good way to learn more about a fund's management is through their communications with shareholders. Many of the world's best money managers take great pride in giving their shareholders semiannual or annual updates on their recent performance, as well as their thoughts on the markets. Some fund manager communications should be required reading, given the insight they provide.

Warren Buffett's letters to shareholders of Berkshire Hathaway are an example. (Although Berkshire is a stock, it has so many companies under its umbrella that it might as well be a fund.) Mr.

Buffett is considered by many to be the greatest investor of all time, and his letters not only reveal the way he thinks, but their candor will also make you laugh. Of course, you may also read a fund manager's letter and get the sense that your investment philosophy doesn't quite mesh. Either way, the more you read, the more you'll know.

Turnover

This is one more aspect of mutual funds you should consider. No, in referring to turnover we're not talking about how many pastries the fund managers eat, but how frequently a fund buys and sells securities.

A fund's turnover rate is expressed as a percentage and can be found in the financial highlights section of the fund's prospectus. The higher the percentage, the greater the fund's buying and selling activity. Since the turnover rate measures annual activity, a rate of 100 percent means that a fund basically changes all of its holdings once a year. A fund with a 200 percent turnover rate would change its entire portfolio about once every six months.

Keep in mind that a higher turnover rate generally indicates a more aggressive manager, one who engages in more frequent buying and selling. However, more aggressive is not necessarily better. In fact, most investors should seek funds with lower turnover ratios. This is because fund managers, like regular investors, must pay commissions on every trade they make. Thus, more frequent trading activity means less of your money stays invested.

In addition, there are less obvious problems with a fund manager making frequent trades, such as the inherent price implications of doing so—for one thing, large buys may boost the price of the stock the fund manager is trying to purchase. The bottom line is that you should seek funds with low turnover rates, unless the fund you're looking at has racked up impressive gains over a number of years. As we've already pointed out, in such cases, investors might be willing to overlook a drawback or two.

Independent Ratings

Of course, even after looking at all of the criteria above, you might still feel apprehensive about investing in a particular fund. For that reason, there are independent agencies that rate mutual funds based on a number of different criteria, including performance and costs.

STANDARD & POOR'S

In addition to providing bond ratings and stock recommendations, Standard & Poor's also provides rankings on more than 11,000 mutual funds. S&P's top fund recommendations are awarded five stars, funds that are moderately attractive are awarded four stars, and so on down to those funds that should be avoided, which are given one star.

MORNINGSTAR

Many individual investors also choose to consult Morningstar, which is widely known for its coverage of the mutual fund industry. Like S&P, Morningstar employs a number of fund analysts who closely track various mutual funds and assign ratings to each.

LIPPER

Although this company's products are somewhat less accessible to individual investors, Lipper provides a large range of data on the mutual fund industry, including special studies and snapshots of specific funds.

Summary

Any investor seeking to purchase a mutual fund should look carefully at a number of areas before buying. The costs of purchasing and owning a fund, including loads and 12b-1 fees, are important to all potential fund owners, even those looking to purchase index funds. Likewise, investors who want to invest in an actively managed fund should examine the fund's prospectus, which will impart information about management as well as its long-term performance history. In the end, getting a second opinion from an independent research house might not be a bad idea either.

PART 5

Retirement Accounts and Other Investments

CHAPTER 12

Retirement Accounts

Retirement—for many of us, it seems so far away. Maybe even for people fairly close to it! However, the truth is that retirement is always creeping up on you, and when it comes time, you're going to want to be prepared.

How best to go about it? By starting early, contributing regularly, and getting your money to work for you. In this chapter, we're going to explore some of the common retirement accounts available, as well as some of the common choices you'll be given.

First Steps to a Sound Retirement

Before we get into specific accounts, let's consider a few general guidelines on retirement accounts.

START

While planning for retirement is something everyone should do, an alarming number of people never get around to opening even one retirement account. According to the Employee Benefit Research Institute, 49 percent of workers with an annual income between $30,000 and $60,000 don't have a retirement account. Of that same group, 30 percent have only a 401(k) account and 12 percent have only an IRA account. Amazingly, only 9 percent of these "middle-income" workers have both a 401(k) and an IRA account.

START EARLY

This point can't be emphasized enough. While opening a retirement account is a positive in itself, the sooner you begin, the better off you'll be. Consider this: A 2001 survey by the Employee Benefit Research Institute revealed that workers aged 21 to 24 participate in employer-sponsored retirement plans at less than half the rate of workers aged 45 to 54 (27.3 versus 65.4 percent). After the example in Chapter 1, the merits of starting early should be manifest. For a slightly different spin, however, here's another example:

Upon starting work at age 25, Al allocated $150 a month to a retirement account. In contrast, Alissa decided to forego contributing until 10 years after Al began. They have both been placing their money in accounts earning an average annual rate of return of 8 percent. By the time they're 65, Al will have an account worth $527,142, while Alissa's account will have grown to $225,044. So, even though Al only contributed $18,000 more than Alissa, his account is now worth an additional $302,098.

ALLOCATE YOUR ASSETS APPROPRIATELY

The same rules of asset allocation we've discussed previously also apply to your retirement accounts. In some respects, nowhere are they more important, since your retirement accounts are by definition a long-term portfolio, one that will likely be the cornerstone of a secure future.

DON'T TOUCH WHAT YOU'VE ALREADY PUT IN

This rule applies to any type of retirement account. As a retirement account grows, it may be tempting to withdraw some money for other purposes. Many people will borrow against what they've saved or will even completely withdraw the funds, promising themselves that they'll replace the amount later. Doing either is generally a mistake. You should treat your retirement account conservatively.

CHOOSE A BENEFICIARY

Although it's not something we like to think about, there's always a possibility of not making it to retirement. You'll want to be prepared for such an event by choosing a beneficiary for your retirement account(s). While this is not difficult, there are a few things you need to keep in mind. The first is that your beneficiary has to be a person or trust. Unfortunately, your poodle can't directly inherit your savings. However, you are entitled to designate more than one beneficiary. To do so, you need to figure out what percentage each entity is entitled to. There are a few other issues, including how your assets will be distributed. To learn more about these, you should consult an attorney or an estate planner.

401(k) Plans

The first retirement account you're likely to see is a company-sponsored 401(k) plan. Although we talked about these accounts earlier, we're going to cover them in greater detail now.

Essentially, a company-sponsored retirement plan lets you contribute some of your pay to an account designated for your retirement. These plans are considered "defined contribution" pension plans since they allow workers to set aside a limited amount of money each year for retirement. The main attraction is that your employer will often match a percentage of what you put in. In addition, the money you contribute is from your pretax pay, which means you're effectively lowering your taxable income. In other words, you pay less in taxes for the time being. Sounds great, doesn't it? It is.

Major Features

Generally, company-sponsored retirement accounts are something to get excited about. However, there are a few major features you'll need to know about before you can decide if you want to participate in one.

WHEN CAN YOU START?

While many companies allow employees to enroll immediately, other plans require that participants be employed for a certain period of time before they're eligible. In some cases it may take a year. The number of hours you work may also play a role. If you can't begin contributing right away, you should make a note of when you can.

DOES YOUR COMPANY MATCH YOUR CONTRIBUTIONS?

If your company doesn't match your contributions, you may also look at IRAs as an alternative. If it does, you'll want to find out the specifics, such as how, at what rate, and to what limit. While most companies will match your contributions with cash, some might use stock instead. If given a choice, it's highly recommended that you opt for cash. Doing so gives you greater freedom and better diversification.

For the most part, investing a substantial portion of money in the company you work for is a mistake. In a sense, your employment there is already a large enough investment. Linking your career and your retirement money to the same ship is a dangerous proposition. For an extreme example of the danger, you need only look to the case of Enron Corporation. Because the energy trader was rewarding employees with stock in their retirement accounts, many people's fortunes were tied to the company's fate. This looked great while the company's stock continued to rise. In fact, many employees were wealthy on paper. But when things took a bad turn, those same employees were left holding the bag. Not only did they lose their jobs, but also their savings.

Figuring out how much money your company will contribute might take a little work. For instance, some companies apply different rates to different contribution amounts. A company might match 100 percent of the first 3 percent of your salary that's contributed, 50 percent of the next 3 percent, and then zero percent of anything above 6 percent. The company might also place a dollar restriction on how much it will contribute; for example, no more than $10,000 a year.

In addition, there are limitations on how much of your own money you're able to contribute. For 2003, you can contribute 1 to 20 percent of your yearly pretax pay to a 401(k) plan, up to the maximum amount of $12,000 ($14,000 if you're 50 or older). However, in some special cases there can be additional restrictions. Also, employers are free to impose lower contribution limits if they so choose. A good place to start investigating your own company's plan is with your human resources department.

You'll also want to know how frequently your company will contribute its share. Although it's common for companies to contribute their portion with every paycheck, some may deposit funds under a different schedule, such as quarterly.

VESTING

Another issue you'll need to check out is whether your company's contributions are subject to a **vesting** period, which determines how long it will take before the money your company contributes becomes yours. If your company's plan has a one-year vesting period, for instance, any money it puts into your retirement account, as well as any money earned on that money, will get taken away from you if you leave the company before the year is up. It's worth noting that in extreme cases it may take up to five years for the money to vest.

Thus, if you only plan on staying at your company for a short time, you shouldn't let its contributions factor into whether you'd like to open a retirement plan there. But rest assured—no matter what the vesting period, any contributions you make to your account, and any money earned on those contributions, are yours to keep no matter what.

Guidelines for 401(k)s

Assuming that you're going to stay with your company until its contributions have vested, there are a few specific guidelines you might want to take into consideration.

CONTRIBUTE THE MAXIMUM AMOUNT THAT'S MATCHED

Although this might seem fairly obvious, many people fail to do so. Perhaps you've seen one of those plexiglass boxes full of money blowing around? If you were inside, you'd likely try to grab as much as you could. You should think of your employer's contributions as "free money" in the same way.

Using the rates we've previously mentioned—100 percent of the first 3 percent, 50 percent of the next 3 percent, and zero percent of anything above 6 percent—would mean that you'd want to contribute at least 6 percent of your total salary to your retirement account. Doing so would get you an immediate 75 percent return on your money. Sometimes it's tempting to only contribute the amount that your company fully matches. The truth is, every extra dollar you put into your retirement account will be a huge help down the road, especially when you consider the power of compounding.

IF YOU CAN, CONTRIBUTE MORE THAN THE MATCHED AMOUNT

You may have other goals, such as saving money to buy a house. If this is the case, then any money over the maximum matched amount may be better put elsewhere. However, if you can contribute more to your company's plan, you should. Why? Because doing so not only further funds your future, but also lowers the amount you're being taxed now. Since the money is being taken out of your salary before taxes, you're effectively lowering your income. While the additional savings may not be monumental, it's just one more reason to aggressively contribute.

Taking Your 401(k) with You

One final thing you may be wondering about company-sponsored 401(k)s is what happens when you leave the company. While the money your company has contributed may or may not go with you, whatever you've contributed is yours no matter what. There's never a vesting period or any other circumstance under which the money you contributed wouldn't be yours.

Even if you're fired, what you've put in is yours. However, you'll probably have a choice to make about where the money is to go. The four main options:

1. Withdraw your money.
2. Leave it with your old employer.
3. Roll it into a new 401(k).
4. Put it into a rollover IRA.

OPTION 1: WITHDRAW YOUR MONEY

Withdrawing the money might sound like a good idea at the time. It's tempting to call it "found money," money best used for shopping sprees, a European vacation, or a new car. But stop right there. These are the same things that you'll want during your retirement, and finding money might be more difficult when you're older.

Withdrawing the money is not advisable. Not only will you endanger your future and all that wonderful compounding interest along the way, but you'll pay for the privilege through taxes and penalties: You'll owe regular income tax on the money you withdraw and, worse, if you're under age $59 \frac{1}{2}$, you'll also face a 10 percent penalty for the early withdrawal.

How does this work in the real world? Say Brenda has $10,000 in her 401(k). The amount seems like just enough to have a good time with, and at the age of 27 she's hardly concerned with retirement yet. However, after she pays state and local taxes on the money, plus the 10 percent early withdrawal penalty, she'll only be left with about $5500 of the initial $10,000. Not quite the amount she was expecting. What would have happened to the money if she'd kept it in a tax-sheltered retirement account? Assuming an annual return of 8 percent, she'd have $54,365 by age 59.

In the end, prematurely withdrawing money from a retirement account just isn't worth it. Luckily, you still have three better options left to choose from.

OPTION 2: LEAVE IT WITH YOUR OLD EMPLOYER

Leaving your money in your old employer's plan might be a good option if the old account offered you a number of good allocation options or if the management fees and expenses were more favorable than the other choices below. However, most companies will require you to have at least $5000 in the 401(k) for it to stay in their plan.

Also, the plan is always subject to change. The things you like about it now might not stay the same. The allocation options may decrease, for one thing, or the fees might become more burdensome. Change is especially likely if your old company merges with another company.

If you decide to leave your 401(k) in an old plan, make sure you continue getting timely information on your account's performance, and always keep the plan up to date with your latest information. In some respects, just the added administrative duties you'll face might make an old 401(k) plan a less attractive option.

OPTION 3: ROLL IT INTO A NEW 401(K)

Rolling your old 401(k) into your new employer's plan will do away with the added hassle of managing a number of accounts. And if the new plan has better features, then transferring your old account is probably the wisest choice. Also, you'd retain the right to borrow against the assets, even though that's not a recommended action.

All this assumes that your new plan accepts rollovers: You'll want to check with your new employer. And if you decide to go with this option, ask that the money be transferred "trustee to trustee." What this means is that it will be sent directly from your last account to your new account—the check never passes through your hands. If you do it any other way, you face a big mess because the government will treat the withdrawal as a "withdrawal" until you prove that the money is actually being put back into a retirement account. The consequence is that 20 percent of the money would be withheld for that year's taxes and you wouldn't get it back until you filed your tax return. Thus, to get all of the money into your new 401(k) immediately, you'd have to take the 20 percent from somewhere else. Here's a real world example:

Michi wants to roll over his old 401(k) plan into his new employer's plan. He has about $30,000 in the old account. Instead of getting the money transferred directly, Michi gets a check from his old employer. But when he receives it, he sees it's only for $24,000. This is because his old employer was obligated to withhold a portion of the money for the year's taxes, in the same way that the employer withheld money from Michi's paychecks. Now, if Michi wants to deposit the full $30,000 into his new account, he only has two choices: find $6000 from somewhere else, or wait until he gets his refund check (up to a year and a half later). Of course, if he waits, he'll be losing a hefty chunk of interest on that $6000.

As you can see, getting a check from your old 401(k) plan makes things unnecessarily sticky. Again, if you're going to go with this option, you're much better off just having the funds sent between the two plan administrators.

OPTION 4: PUT IT INTO A ROLLOVER IRA

Of course, you have yet another option: the rollover IRA. This is a specific type of Individual Retirement Account created to give people another way of keeping their old 401(k) money invested for retirement.

We'll cover IRA accounts below. Suffice it to say here that there are a number of advantages to the rollover IRA, including the fact that it provides a virtually unlimited number of investment options. You can purchase specific stocks or pick from any of the various funds out there. In addition, you'll probably get better information on your account, since federal law requires detailed disclosure on IRA accounts.

IRAs

Individual Retirement Accounts are an extremely popular way to save for retirement. In fact, according to the Investment Company Institute, as of 2001 about 42 percent of U.S. households owned IRAs. There are a few different types of IRAs to choose from, including the traditional IRA, which is a tax-deductible type, and the Roth IRA, which is nondeductible. All IRAs offer you the ability to invest your money in a wide assortment of assets, including individual stocks. Where they differ is on who may contribute and how taxes will be assessed.

The deductible versus nondeductible thing refers to what type of money you're putting into the account. Deductible IRAs are funded by the equivalent of pretax dollars, like most 401(k)s. In other words, you can deduct the contributions you make when it comes time to file your income tax. Nondeductible IRAs are comprised of money that has already been taxed, so you can't deduct the contributions. However, the interest you earn on the nondeductible money might be tax-free, while taxes on the interest you earn in a deductible IRA are merely deferred until withdrawal. It's sort of a pay-now or pay-later issue.

At first it might be hard to understand how a nondeductible IRA holds any advantage over a regular account. After all, isn't paying later usually bad? The trick is in the timing. People with traditional IRAs are counting on earning less in their old age. That way, when they begin withdrawing their money, it will be taxed at a lower rate than it would while they're still in their peak earning years.

Let's lay out a comparison to demonstrate the differences between a regular account, a tax-deferred account, and a Roth IRA. We'll begin with the supposition that you have $3000 to contribute to an account, and we'll say that each account earns 10 percent annually. Further, we'll assume a tax rate of 31 percent. Of course, you'll have less money to put into the Roth because the dollars are after taxes. Plus, you'd be able to deduct the money you contributed to the regular IRA. So, where does that leave you? It would look like Table 12-1.

TABLE 12-1. Comparing Regular Accounts, Traditional IRA, and Roth IRA

	Regular Account	Traditional IRA	Roth IRA
Contribution	$3,000	$3,000	$2,070
Tax Deduction	$0	$930	$0
Total Payment	$3,000	$2,070	$2,070
Value 20 Years Later	$11,394	$20,183.00	$13,926
Tax on Withdrawal	$0	$6,257	$0
Money Left	$11,394	$13,926	$13,926

After 20 years, the regular account, which we're assuming gets taxed annually, will be worth $11,394. After paying $6257 in taxes, the traditional IRA will be worth $13,926. And after paying nothing in taxes, the Roth IRA will be worth . . . $13,926.

At this point you're probably wondering what's up. After all, the Roth posed no advantage over the traditional account. Well, first, remember that everyone's individual situation is different. The upfront tax deduction may or may not be that beneficial to you. Also, the greater freedom that the Roth offers when it's time to withdraw is an intangible benefit for many people. More on this in a minute, though. Last, keep in mind that our above example wasn't necessarily how things operate in the real world.

Because everyone's situation is unique, it's difficult to recommend the best route for you to take. However, for most people the Roth IRA is the preferred choice. Why? Because it's a completely tax-sheltered investment account. In other words, it allows your investments to earn interest without requiring you to pay taxes on the money you've made. It also gives you greater freedom when it comes time to withdraw your money.

Table 12-2 provides a quick breakdown of the differences between a traditional IRA and a Roth IRA.

TABLE 12-2. Traditional IRA and Roth IRA

	Traditional IRA	Roth IRA
Contributions	Tax Deductible	Not Deductible
Earnings on Contributions	Taxes Deferred	Never Taxed
Begin Withdrawing	Age 70 1/2	Never Mandatory

Because the Roth IRA is probably the better choice for you, it's worth looking at in greater detail.

The Roth IRA

Named after former Senator William Roth from Delaware, the Roth IRA became available to qualified participants on January 1, 1998. As with most things, the Roth IRA has a number of rules surrounding it. Many of these relate to participation eligibility. First, you must have income to contribute to a Roth IRA. Specifically, you're allowed to contribute the lesser of $3000 or your wages for a given year. Confused? What this means is that if you only made $1000 last year, that's all you can contribute to a Roth IRA. If you made $20,000, you can only put in $3000.

One exception to this rule is that married couples with only one person working may each contribute $3000 to their individual accounts. So, if Joe and Jaime are married, but only Joe works, both Joe and Jaime may each contribute $3000 to their respective Roth IRAs.

And while you can have as many IRA accounts as you'd like, the maximum contribution rate is a total applied to all of your accounts, not each one individually. This means if you have 30 different IRAs, you may only put $100 in each of them for any given year. Keep in mind, the contribution rate was raised to $3000 for 2002. Before that, the limit was only $2000. Fortunately, it's slated to continue rising, to $4000 in 2005 and $5000 in 2008. And if you're over 50, you're in luck since as of 2002 you can contribute an extra $500 a year in what's known as a "catch-up provision."

Additional restrictions on who can contribute to a Roth IRA are based on how much a person makes—specifically, their adjusted gross income. Luckily, your contributions to other retirement plans, such as a 401(k), have no bearing on your eligibility. There are a number of different designations, based on the different ways that you can file your taxes.

The designations are (a) individual filing singly, (b) married filing jointly, and (c) married filing separately. Each designation has its own set of cutoff points, with most people permitted to contribute the maximum, some allowed to contribute a portion of the maximum amount, and some unable to contribute at all. Essentially, if you're filing singly and making less than $100,000 a year, it's almost definite that you can contribute the maximum amount. If you're married and filing jointly, you and your spouse will have to have a combined adjusted gross income of less than $150,000 to put in the full amount. And if you're married and filing separately, your contributions will almost definitely be limited, if allowed at all.

If you ever find yourself only allowed a partial contribution, it might be helpful to know that the amount you're permitted to contribute decreases in a manner that's inversely proportional to the size of your adjusted gross income (below the final cutoff). However, once your contribution has been chopped down to $200, its next stop is zero. In other words, unless you're completely barred from contributing, you'll always be allowed to at least put in $200.

It's also important to know that you can contribute to a Roth IRA between January 1 of that tax year and the April 15 of the following year—up until you file your tax return for that year. The best-case scenario is to contribute the full amount in the beginning of a given year. That way you can reap the maximum benefit of compounding interest in a tax-sheltered account. However, if you wait until the period between January and April of the following year, be sure to let your account **custodian**—the firm responsible for your account—know what year your contribution should go toward. Not doing so can result in a real IRS headache later.

Now that you know a little more about how to put money into a Roth, you might be wondering how and when you can get your money back out of one. As noted earlier, the Roth IRA gives you greater freedom when it's time to withdraw your money. In fact, because the money you've put in has already been taxed, you're never obligated to withdraw it. This alone can make the Roth IRA especially useful for estate planning purposes, since it allows someone to directly pass along a tax-sheltered portfolio to an heir. The traditional IRA differs in this respect because it requires an account holder to begin taking withdrawals by age $70^{1/2}$.

Don't forget that the distributions you do take from a Roth IRA won't be subject to taxation. Distributions from a regular IRA would be. Therefore, your adjusted gross income during retirement will get a boost.

Defined Benefit Pension Funds

Although many companies have moved away from providing their employees with defined benefit pensions upon retirement, opting instead to let employees participate in things like 401(k) plans, some employers continue to set aside money for their workers' futures along with the guarantee that after employment for a specified number of years, a retired employee will receive a set amount of money every year for life. Generally, large, established companies offer these plans.

The basic idea behind a pension fund is simple. In fact, you can almost think of them as private mutual funds for companies (see Chapters 10 and 11 if you need to refresh your memory on funds). Pension funds are run as separate investment portfolios, generally under the watchful eyes of professional money managers. A pension fund is considered a trust fund for qualifying retirees. Most, if not all, pension funds are made up of both stocks and bonds, with a common allocation being 60 percent in stocks and 40 percent in fixed income.

Just like many investors, a company will typically contribute a portion of money to its pension fund every year. How much it decides to contribute is calculated using a complicated formula. Some of the factors that go into the decision include how much money is already in the fund; how many employees are near, or in, retirement; and how much the portfolio is expected to increase over the next year.

For the most part, a pension fund isn't something you'll need to concern yourself with. If your company offers one, it will outline everything you need to know. One important point to be on the lookout for, however, is how long you'll have to stay with your company in order to qualify for the retirement package. Often, the amount of money you receive during retirement from the company's pension fund will vary depending on how long you worked there.

There are a number of other retirement accounts that may be available to you, depending on where you work. For example, many state governments offer their employees special programs. However, you should still look for the same characteristics in any plan that might be available to you. These include investment flexibility, tax benefits, and "free money" features like matched contributions.

Summary

Although retirement may seem a long way off, the earlier you start planning for it, the better off you'll be. Even if you never plan on retiring, the advantages of IRAs and matched 401(k)s are too great to pass up. Many of these plans provide investors with tax incentives, great investment choices, and, best of all, a disciplined way to save for the future.

CHAPTER 13

Scams: Investments to Avoid

So far, the investment options we've discussed serve different purposes for different investment goals. However, just as it's important to understand what to invest in, it's also important to understand what *not* to invest in. In this chapter we'll point out some typical temptations you may find yourself faced with along the road of investing.

First, let's reiterate a few points we made elsewhere: The two most important factors in determining which investments make sense for you are your goals and the level of risk you're willing to take on. It's the latter that most concerns us here. This chapter will demonstrate that some things are so risky, they're just not right for anyone.

Penny Stocks

Perhaps the most common way that both new and seasoned investors lose money is through the purchase of highly speculative (but legitimate) investments like penny stocks. Some of these stocks do in fact become bigger and better-known, but the number of failures greatly outweighs the number of winners.

The truly unfortunate thing about these stocks is that they're usually thinly traded. In other words, few shares change hands on a daily basis. This allows any buying or selling interest to greatly affect the stock's price. Couple that with the fact that information on many of these companies is hard to come by and you have a recipe for disaster.

The allure of penny stocks is that they're usually very cheap, which makes them easy for any investor to purchase. In addition, since they are priced so cheaply, it's easy for investors to imagine their $1000 investment doubling many times over. Many justify the risk by saying something like, "Hey, it's only $1000. People lose that much at Las Vegas. Besides, what's $1000 anyway?" The answer is that $1000 is precisely one thousand dollars, a sum that many of the same people who employ this logic would love to have for some other purpose.

The typical story with penny stock scams is always the same. A person, or a few people, quietly accumulate a large amount of stock. Since the price will be relatively cheap, it doesn't take much to build up a position. Once the stock has been accumulated, these same people, or their associates, will begin drumming up interest in the stock. This can be done in a number of ways, although word of mouth typically plays a large role once the momentum has begun.

The Internet has only made the process easier and faster. Scammers often use message boards or "free research" e-mails as ways of initially getting investors interested. Usually, they'll pass along false information to increase the proposition of investing in an otherwise worthless company. A common ploy is to tout a new development that is supposedly in the works—a new product, a big contract, a buyout; all of these are perfect fodder. As people pass along this "hot tip," more investors get interested. Meanwhile, this burst of enthusiasm creates stronger-than-normal demand for the stock. Thus, the price rises.

People who got into the stock early, even those uninvolved in the scam, may very well be able to reap large profits. Of course, this adds fuel to the fire since people further down the line see that their friends—the ones recommending the stock—have already made profits (if only on paper). Then one day the demand dries up, the people who began the feeding frenzy have sold all of their shares at a tidy profit, and those who are still holding the shares watch the stock price fall as everyone hurries to get out.

Sounds simple, right? It is. Unfortunately, it's also very effective. This scam, in one form or another, has been played out more times than you can imagine. And it will happen over and over again in the future.

So what can you do to protect yourself?

CONSIDER THE SOURCE OF AN INVESTMENT RECOMMEN-DATION. If it's from a friend, find out the source, then do some research on your own. If you get a recommendation from an e-mail or on a message board, do some research on your own. Heck, even if your mother is a stockbroker and she gives you an investment idea—do some research on your own.

TREAT EVERYTHING SKEPTICALLY. Just because someone you know has made a lot of money from a stock, doesn't mean that you will too. This leads us to . . .

RESIST PEER PRESSURE. It sounds funny, doesn't it? Surprisingly, peer pressure often plays a huge part in these silly scams. Why? Because people feel better about their own decisions when others agree with them. This is human nature. And while peer pressure can sometimes be present latently, it will often be more overt. Consider this example:

A bunch of 50-year-old guys are on a golf trip in Myrtle Beach. They begin talking stocks. One of the guys in the group starts bragging about how much money he's made in penny stocks. He then tells the other golfers about a stock he's currently buying. He's confident it's going to triple within a few weeks. Most of the other guys become interested and start calling their brokers. One of the golfers, although tempted to just plunk down the money ("What's $1000?"), decides to call for a second opinion. The next day, he tells the other guys that he's not going to buy any. The other guys begin calling him "chicken." These are grown men, mind you. Of course, the story ends with a bit of vindication since all of those other golfers ended up losing most of their investments shortly thereafter. Think it doesn't happen? It happened to my dad. Fortunately, he was the chicken.

A corollary to the rule above might be: *resist greed.* Greed is perhaps the strongest motivator. As an investor, greed is not your friend. In fact, when coupled with peer pressure, it can be downright dangerous. Greed is the very force that drives investment scams. It's what the empty promises of outsized gains thrive on. Still not convinced? Read on.

The Ponzi Scheme

The penny stock scam is just an iteration of a larger model: the Ponzi scheme. No, Ponzi wasn't that cool guy on *Happy Days*. To his investors, he was anything but cool. Charles Ponzi came to America from Italy early in the 20th century and eventually established himself as one of the premier "bankers" of New England. He began attracting investors by claiming he'd found a way to cash in on a pricing discrepancy between postage stamps from different countries. While what Ponzi suggested was at least theoretically possible, it's unlikely that he ever did much stamp trading. Instead, he simply paid his longer-standing investors with newer investors' money. While Ponzi was eventually arrested (it wasn't the first time), many of the people who invested in his enterprise never saw a dime.

Ponzi scams are also known as "pyramid schemes," since they basically revolve around someone at the top getting rich from the people on the bottom. Let's stick with postage-related concepts. Have you ever gotten one of those chain letters that promises bad luck if you don't pass it along to 10 friends? Well, even these chain letters have been used in money-making schemes.

In this version, you receive a letter containing a list. All you have to do is send a dollar to each person on the list, then you cross off a name, add yours, and send the updated list to a bunch of your friends. The idea is that in no time people all over the country will be sending you money back. Anyone with a bit of common sense can see the disconnect here: If the idea continues to be carried out, it will only result in an infinite array of people sending each other money. People who realize this still participate, though. Why? Because they figure they won't be the ones left holding the bag. Even if it wasn't illegal (according to postal regulations, it is), it's foolish and hardly qualifies as an investment. Or does it?

A few modern day adaptations of this scheme are still being played out all over the country. Only instead of using a dollar to play, they require thousands. The most obvious descendant goes like this:

A man comes to town with a great new investment plan. A few of you will give him $2000 to join his investment group. Next, you'll go out and recruit a few friends to join. Of course, they'll pay part of the fee to you and part to the guy who recruited you. In turn, they'll be able to recruit some of their friends and family into the club.

This will continue for some time. Like the penny stock scams, some people will be raking in the dough along the way. Despite warnings from their more logical counterparts, the profits encourage more people to join. These new recruits scoff at the skeptics. They point to the checks their friends, acquaintances, and coworkers have been getting. Eventually, it gets harder to recruit more people to join. In other words, the supply of fools in the town has run dry. When that happens, many of those who contributed still haven't received anywhere near what they put it. Then people at the bottom sue the people they've given money to. Investigations ensue. And the founder of the club, who's been collecting money from everyone in the club, is probably halfway to Barbados by the time anyone even catches on.

I know, this one sounds so obvious that it's impossible to believe. Guess again. One group that I know of consisted of teachers, accountants, and a number of other people who should have known better. Too bad they didn't.

One last example, which is almost as unreasonable:

A recent college grad says she plans on cashing out her Roth IRA because she's found "a better investment." When prompted, she says she's found an investor who promises her a 10 percent return on her investment . . . every month! That's right, for a minimum investment of $2000 (seems to be the magic number, eh?), this investor will send her a monthly check in the amount of $200, or she can simply choose to have her profits reinvested.

The promise of a return of 10 percent annually is reason enough for pause. But 10% a month? It sounds too good to be true, doesn't it? That's because it is! Should you ever find yourself confronted with such an offer, take a step back and apply a little common sense. Even if there were an investment that could consistently return 10 percent a month, why would someone want to tell you about it? Of course, simple logic is often not enough to dissuade someone in such a situation. In fact, they will usually be looking for reasons to participate. Greed is a strong force, indeed.

The most common way of rationalizing participation is by pointing to the fact that other investors have already been receiving payments. However, in most cases those investors will only have been participating for a few months. A potential investor might also say something like, "But I've already met the man in person." The fact that there's a living human being behind it all is supposed to justify the fact that the whole thing is real. In reality, the only thing it proves is that it's possible to lie to someone's face. Remember that many people's houses have been robbed by familiar faces.

While the goal here is not to harden your heart toward your fellow human beings, the odds are good that this situation will end up being yet another version of the classic Ponzi scheme. And as an investor, it's always wise to have the odds in your favor.

Of course, the best part of this particular scam is that most people will opt to reinvest their profits. At 10 percent a month, who wouldn't? That way, when the scammer decides to pull the plug and head to Fiji, he takes all of the money with him. Depending on the way the agreement was written, he may even just claim that an investment went sour and that all of the money given to him has been lost.

Summary

While there are a tremendous number of investment scams out there, the general idea is always the same. If an investment sounds remarkably better than anything else you've come across, it's probably remarkably riskier too. In fact, it's likely to be a scam. The market for investments is self-regulating—profitable ones attract demand, which boosts the price and lowers the effective return. If you think you're one of the few people to have stumbled upon something magnificent, you're probably not. This is not to say that profitable opportunities won't present themselves from time to time. Just don't expect them to provide you with 10 percent a month.

CHAPTER 14

Doing Well in a Bad Market

In many respects, readers of this book may be more fortunate than many of their peers, even those who have already been investing for the last decade or so. But experience will always remain the best teacher, and since the wisest people manage to learn from the experiences of others, no current book for new investors would be complete without a look back on how the stock market—or more accurately, the sum of stock market investors—behaved in the 1990s and at the start of the new millennium. By doing so, you'll get a better understanding of just how volatile, profitable, and, yes, dangerous the markets can get. In addition, we'll talk later in this section about what specific strategies often work especially well during difficult market periods.

By most accounts, the greatest bull market in American financial history began in 1982. Sure, there were bumps along the way, including the crash of 1987. However, through the rearview mirror, even that dark day was just another downward blip in an otherwise upward trend. By the time the 1990s were half over, individual stock ownership in the United States was near its highest point ever. More importantly, technological advances were fueling a number of changes, including higher productivity. Economically, inflation remained tame and interest rates were reasonable. Many new companies were sprouting up, awash in money and promising tremendously strong growth. It was a good time to own stocks.

People began speaking of a "New Economy," a utopia where growth was infinite, a place where investments were evaluated less by earnings and tangible assets and more by things like potential.

Arguably, at this point, it actually became a bad time to own stocks, especially those that were in favor at the time. Why? Because what followed was a heightened state of interest in owning stock in companies, especially technology companies, which saw investors willing to pay exorbitant prices for little more than a name and a shabby business plan.

Even the shares of many companies that were profitable became outrageously pricey, premised on the belief that their profits would continue to increase at such a rapid pace that the premium prices were justified. In short, it was a time of rabid speculation in the stock market. And with every market upshot, more investors flooded the market with fresh cash.

One of the worst side effects of the feeding frenzy was that many investors abandoned the notion of a diversified portfolio, opting instead to chase outsized gains through ownership of only the highest-flying stocks. In fact, an oft-cited approach was to own a portfolio full of companies specializing in "converging technologies." Admittedly, it sounded impressive. Yet what it boiled down to was owning stock in a number of interdependent companies, akin to owning a cheese factory, a tomato farm, a warehouse full of dough, and 15 pizza shops. Sure, when people are eating pizzas, this strategy works well. But what happens when falafels become the next big thing? Essentially, by the end of 2000, people were sick of metaphorical pizza and a lot of investors were left holding empty boxes.

In addition, the economy looked weaker. As was to be expected, the market began working off the indulgences of the late 1990s. And it wasn't pretty. Many investors had become so used to profitably **buying the dips**—adding to their stock positions at every downward market move—that they found it hard to resist continuing the habit. And for short periods of time, the market headed back up. But overall, the highs got lower, and so did the lows. Then came the terrorist attacks of September 11, which brought a new load of uncertainties.

By the middle of 2002, the Nasdaq composite was off its high by about 70 percent and the S&P 500 was down more than 40 percent. And the losses carried over into the early part of 2003. Many people watched as their retirement accounts shrunk. Major bankruptcies ensued. Adding insult to injury, a number of company executives became the subject of investigations for profiting as their companies floundered. Investors felt badly burned. The losses fostered additional selling, just as previous gains had spurred more buying throughout the late '90s.

Such is the way of markets: They tend to overshoot their marks on the way up and on the way down. And in what may be some sort of cosmic harmony, a lot of good news accompanies the fat times, just as a slew of negative news shows up in time for the fall.

So, what might new investors learn from the latest block of stock market history? They might note that, like most good things, the stock market party started in celebration of legitimate events—tame inflation, high productivity—and a time of fervent technological and business advancements. Yet, like many good parties, it soon got out of hand.

Through a confluence of greed, media hype, and reckless abandon, investors became willing to accept the most dreaded of phrases: "This time it will be different." In fact, so strong was the herd mentality that the few disbelievers left hanging around were scorned. Even the venerable Warren Buffett was declared a has-been when he refused to drink from the punch bowl.

Herein lies a good indicator that things have gotten out of hand. Whenever opinion becomes so obviously lopsided, you would be wise to look more closely at the reasoning, if any, behind such opinions. In addition, investors should periodically look at their own reasons for doing things, with extra attention toward ferreting out extreme levels of greed or fear. While introspection of this sort is no easy task, a little self-examination goes a long way. And common sense? Well, it's invaluable.

Of course, disciplined investors can further remove the risk of temptation by adhering to the strategies discussed in this book— namely, by outlining their goals, developing a plan, diversifying their holdings, and allocating additional assets over time.

Still, it might be helpful to look at some strategies that are commonly employed during expected periods of prolonged economic uncertainty or market instability. Although the decision to actively shift in and out of investments in the hope of timing the market is best left alone by most investors, people with higher risk tolerances or more aggressive goals may benefit from considering some of these concepts in the future. At the least, they will better help you understand common modes of thinking during tough times. Besides, some of these ideas work well in any market.

Dividend Paying Stocks

During turbulent markets, stocks that pay healthy dividends generally hold up better than those that don't. One reason for this is because stocks that pay dividends tend to be stable companies with ample profits. As such, they're inherently better able to weather tough economic conditions. Also, since individual stock prices are less likely to go up during down markets, investors like knowing that the dividend will still provide them with a return on their investment.

Throughout the first few years of the new millennium, dividend payers certainly held up better than their nonpaying brethren (see Table 14-1).

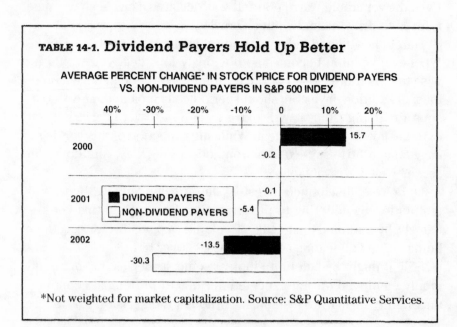

TABLE 14-1. Dividend Payers Hold Up Better

AVERAGE PERCENT CHANGE* IN STOCK PRICE FOR DIVIDEND PAYERS VS. NON-DIVIDEND PAYERS IN S&P 500 INDEX

*Not weighted for market capitalization. Source: S&P Quantitative Services.

Real Estate Investment Trusts

REITs are companies that own, operate, and rent properties. By law, these special corporations are required to distribute 90 percent of their profits to their shareholders. Because of this, REITs generally provide investors with substantial dividends.

In a sense, they're a variation on the dividend-paying theme above. However, the fact that REITs are most influenced by the real estate market somewhat insulates them from weakness in other areas. As a result, these investments work especially well when real estate remains strong, as it did throughout 2001 and 2002. During that time, many real estate markets continued to perform well despite a weak economy and a sagging stock market.

Homebuilding Stocks

As we noted above, sometimes real estate remains strong during poor economic times. During these times, many investors look to own stocks of companies that construct and sell new homes. Of course, if the real estate market begins to wane, these stocks are likely to underperform.

Gold Stocks

Although it doesn't hold the same significance it once did, to many investors, gold continues to provide a haven during tough times (see gold funds, Chapter 10). Since buying and selling the metal itself becomes a difficult task, many people turn to the stocks of companies that engage in mining, refining, and selling gold. Of course, the nature of this line of business is highly speculative. Therefore, it's important these stocks be thoroughly investigated before purchase.

Consumer Staples

When the economy sours, it's common for people to curb their spending. Many forgo new car purchases or luxurious vacations. However, most people continue to brush their teeth and wash their clothes. Companies that fall under the consumer staples banner are responsible for producing and selling the goods that people don't generally live without. Many of these stocks are good long-term buy and hold candidates since their businesses are less cyclical than most others.

Pharmaceutical Stocks

Although a number of changes in the pharmaceutical industry have made these stocks less stable than they used to be, the same philosophy that applies to consumer staples stocks also applies here. Even during tough times, people take their medicine. So, the shares of companies that make and sell medicines generally enjoy profit growth during good and bad times.

Utilities

At one time, these stocks were called "widow and orphan stocks" since their returns were so stable. However, as with pharmaceutical companies, changes in the industry have lessened the predictability of earnings from utilities. Still, many of these companies will provide their investors with good returns regardless of economic weakness. Many of them continue to have healthy dividend payouts, especially those that derive a large portion of their revenues from regulated utility operations.

Defense Contractors

Defense contractors are the private companies that build the technologies and weaponry used by our military forces. Although they are not necessarily stable, a large part of their revenue comes from big government contracts. So, their income streams aren't subject to the whim of the financial markets. They can provide good returns during political instability, which is otherwise bad for the stock market.

Other Havens

Other groups that do well include tobacco companies, as well as both alcoholic and nonalcoholic beverage companies. Also, restaurant stocks, which technically fall into the consumer discretionary category—i.e., the first things people stop buying when money gets tight—have shown promise during tough times too. This may be because Americans are eating out more, in good times and bad; often, eating out is simply the cheapest and fastest way to fulfill one of those basic human needs. Finally, a number of value-oriented retailers tend to do well even in adverse conditions, as people look especially hard for bargains during tough times.

Of course, many investors decide to completely cash out their stock holdings during prolonged market downturns. For some, this might be a good idea. However, for investors with longer time horizons, the move to other assets might be a mistake. This is because, historically, every bear market has ended with swift and pronounced gains. It's been said before: With proper asset allocation, a long-term investment strategy will generally take care of itself.

But say you wanted to move into more defensive assets altogether . . . where might you look?

For many individual investors, the most common place would be one of the accounts we covered in Chapter 1: CDs, savings accounts, or money markets.

Money markets are a particularly good example. Often, as the market falls, the collective value of American money markets skyrockets. Much of the deposits come from stock sales, as most brokerage houses offer money markets as a temporary place to hold funds. This cash is known as money "on the sidelines," since it will presumably be reinvested in the stock market when things look more promising.

Many market pundits will cite high levels of cash waiting for deployment in their prognostications for market recoveries. Of course, other money flows into money market accounts when investors choose to change the way they allocate their retirement contributions. In these cases, it's even harder to tell whether the funds will be used for future stock purchases. Many investors also become more interested in other so-called "safe havens" when stocks head south. Popular choices include the gamut of bonds—Treasuries, municipals, TIPS, and I Bonds—and other more tangible things like real estate.

The irony of the "flight to quality" that ensues during a stock market malaise is that many of the assets investors begin considering should have been in their portfolios all along. In addition, by constantly chasing the best performers, these people often do themselves more harm than good, by cashing out underperforming assets and reinvesting in soon-to-be underperforming assets.

Summary

Investors can learn a lot from the market's rise and fall in the late 1990s. Namely, that time period only proved the value of a long-term, well-diversified investment strategy. Similarly, to do well in a tough market environment, perhaps your best bet is to stick to your long-term investing plan and let the turbulence work for you.

Conclusion

Through this book, you've learned about some basic investments and how to begin researching them. Of course, your path has just begun. There is a lot more to learn.

The financial markets are more complicated than ever these days—full of thrice-removed derivatives, 24-hour-a-day exchanges, and live television coverage of every market uptick. In addition, you will undoubtedly encounter times of despair, when it seems as though the entire system has been designed to rob you of your hard-earned money. And there will be good days, too. Days when you're sure you'll be retiring within two weeks.

My advice is to ignore both the good days and the bad days. And definitely ignore the television coverage—it will only amplify your feelings.

If you want to build wealth, the best thing you can do is develop a plan and stick to it. The best plans involve spending less than you make, and putting the difference into something that is likely to increase in value over time. And over the last hundred years, stocks have outpaced other investments, including beds (so-called "mattress funds"), bonds, and beachfront property. Of course, as you'll often hear, past performance doesn't guarantee future results. It's true. In the end, self-control, a level head, and a long-term outlook are probably even more important than seeking out every last percentage point gain. Time works wonders if you just let it.

Seek out investment advice not only from the sources given in Appendix A, but also from your local newspaper or that special-interest magazine that you have lying around. Read everything that you can get your hands on. The best investment ideas won't come from a guy in a pinstripe suit, unless you've already got a few million dollars ready for deployment. On second thought, even if you are a millionaire, your best investment ideas are still unlikely to come from a guy in a pinstripe suit.

Remember that an investment is more than a piece of paper. When you buy a stock, you are not betting on red or black. You are purchasing a stake in a company. If you pick your stocks with this understanding, your odds are far better than 18 out of 38. Likewise, when you buy a bond, you are loaning money to some entity. If you believe that entity will pay you back, you are making a sound investment. No investment is a certainty; however, some investments are more certain than others. As an investor, it is your job to discern and use these differences.

There are a lot of sharks in the sea of investments. Fortunately, common sense is a wonderful shark repellant. Ask questions, be suspicious, and avoid guaranteed returns. Remember, no investment is a certainty—only death and taxes fall into that category. If you are successful in your investments, your heirs can look forward to your death; you can all look forward to the taxes. Still, may you be successful in your investments.

APPENDIX:

Investing Resources

Books

David M. Blitzer. *Outpacing the Pros: Using Indexes to Beat Wall Street's Savviest Money Managers.* McGraw-Hill.

John C. Bogle. *Bogle on Mutual Funds.* Irwin Professional Publishing.

Benjamin Mark Cole. *The Pied Pipers of Wall Street.* Bloomberg Press.

Bradford Cornell. *The Equity Risk Premium.* John Wiley & Sons.

Sidney Cottle, Roger F. Murray, and Frank E. Block. *Graham and Dodd's Security Analysis.* McGraw-Hill.

Charles D. Ellis, editor, with James R. Vertin. *Classics . . . An Investor's Anthology.* Dow-Jones-Irwin.

Benjamin Graham. *The Intelligent Investor.* Harpercollins.

Robert G. Hargstrom. *The Warren Buffet Portfolio.* John Wiley & Sons.

Joseph Lisanti and Joseph Tigue. *The Dividend Rich Investor.* McGraw-Hill.

Peter Lynch, with John Rothchild. *One Up on Wall Street.* Penguin Books.

Burton G. Malkiel. *A Random Walk Down Wall Street.* W.W. Norton & Co.

Robert Natale. *Fast Stocks, Fast Money.* McGraw-Hill.

William J. O'Neil. *How to Make Money in Stocks.* McGraw-Hill.

James P. O'Shaughnessy. *What Works on Wall Street.* McGraw-Hill.

Jeremy J. Siegel. *Stocks for the Long Run.* Irwin Professional Publishing.

John Train. *The Money Masters.* HarperCollins.

Magazines

Barron's
Business Week
The Economist
Forbes
Fortune
Kiplinger's

Newspapers

Financial Times
Investor's Business Daily
Wall Street Journal

Websites

www.aaii.org Site of American Association for Individual Investors. Includes various educational features.

www.bloomberg.com Business-related news site.

www.briefing.com Various investment-related information, including timely market news.

www.businessweek.com Website of *Business Week* magazine, which includes a number of features from Standard & Poor's.

www.cboe.com Website of the Chicago Board Options Exchange. Contains a wealth of information on options.

www.cbsmarketwatch.com Business-related news site.

www.cnbc.com Business-related news site.

www.cnnfn.com Business-related news site.

www.fool.com Home of the Motley Fool. Great website for both beginning and experienced investors.

www.ici.org Investment Company Institute site. Provides information on mutual funds.

www.moneychimp.com Investing site, which includes online calculators and explanations of investment concepts.

www.nasd.com National Association of Securities Dealers site. Contains information on registered investment professionals, including past histories.

www.nasdaq-amex.com Official site of the Nasdaq Stock Market and the American Stock Exchange.

www.nyse.com Official site of the New York Stock Exchange. Includes neat features like the virtual trading floor.

www.outlookonline.com Standard & Poor's flagship investment advisory newsletter in an online format. Contains commentary, analysis, and portfolios. Visit for a free 30-day trial.

www.quicken.com Information and tools related to investments and taxes.

www.sec.gov Securities and Exchange Commission site. Loads of information on securities laws and recent company filings.

www.siliconinvestor.com Stock research site with very active and knowledgeable message boards.

www.standardandpoors.com Standard & Poor's corporate website. Information on the company's products and services, including data on its indexes and recent credit ratings.

www.thestreet.com Investing site with free and premium sections. Lots of food for thought.

www.wsrn.com Wall Street Research Net site, which allows investors to research public companies.

www.yahoo.com Web portal with an extremely popular financial section. Message boards, news, research, etc.

Glossary

Adjusted gross income. An income figure computed when calculating taxes. It is based on gross income, less any business expenses and deductions like retirement account contributions or alimony.

Angel investors. Investors who fund enterprises during their earliest stage of development. Angel investors are often wealthy individuals.

Annual percentage rate. The cost of credit paid to the lender, expressed as a simple percentage.

Arbitrage. The act of benefiting from differences in price of the same commodity, currency, or security traded on two or more markets. The arbitrageur makes money by selling in one market while simultaneously buying in another market.

Asset allocation. The percentage that each investment class represents within the overall composition of an investor's portfolio.

Balanced fund. A mutual fund that invests in a mix of bonds, stocks, and cash. It attempts to blend asset classes to produce a conservative growth and income portfolio.

Balance sheet. An itemized financial statement that shows the assets, liabilities, and net worth of a company on a specific date

Basis point. One one-hundredth of a percentage point; a percent equals 100 basis points.

Bear market. A prolonged period of stagnant or falling stock prices.

Beta. A measure of the volatility of a stock or stock fund's price relative to the general market.

Blue chips. Stocks of large, stable, well-known public companies. The term comes from high-value gambling markers.

Bond. A bond represents a debt, or an IOU, from an issuing entity to a bondholder.

Book value. A company's total assets minus its total liabilities. In other words, how much a company would be worth in the event of liquidation.

Bull market. A prolonged period of increasing stock prices.

Callable bonds. Bonds with a provision allowing the issuer to retire the bond before its maturity date.

Call option. A security that gives an owner the right to buy shares of an underlying asset at a specific price for a certain fixed period of time.

Capitalization. The value of a public corporation based on the market price of its issued and outstanding common stock, expressed in millions.

Cash flow. Accounting definitions of cash flow vary. A popular one is net income plus depreciation and amortization, which are noncash charges against earnings.

Certificate of deposit. CDs are safer, longer-term investments that require the deposit of a certain amount of money in exchange for a fixed-rate of return.

Churning. The practice of frequently buying and selling investments. Can be employed by investment professionals to increase the commissions assessed to a client.

Closed-end fund. An investment fund with a limited number of shares outstanding. Closed-end funds are traded on exchanges or over-the-counter, and should not be confused with open-end funds that may be closed (unavailable) to new investors. (See *open-end fund.*)

Commission. The fee charged by a broker for buying or selling an investment.

Common stock. Shares of stock that come with regular voting rights. Second to preferred shares in terms of dividends and asset distributions.

Compounding interest. Phenomenon of interest being earned on top of interest already earned.

Consensus estimate. The average earnings number expected by professional analysts who follow that particular company.

Convertible bond. A bond with a provision allowing it to be converted into stock under certain circumstances.

Cost basis. The average price paid for a particular investment. Used to calculate the overall gain or loss on a particular holding.

Covered call. Writing a call option when the underlying stock is owned.

Credit risk. Credit risk represents the possibility that an issuer of a financial obligation will not be able to repay interest and principal on a timely basis.

Current ratio. A company's current assets divided by its current liabilities.

Day order. A stock order that can only be filled during the current trading day. If it is not filled, it's cancelled at the end of that day.

Derivatives. Financial instruments that are based upon other investments. See *Options* and *Futures*.

Discount brokerage. A brokerage house that offers only basic trading services, but charges cheaper commissions.

Diversification. Placing money across a wide variety of investment types.

Dollar cost averaging. An investment strategy that entails buying a set dollar amount of an investment on a regular basis, usually monthly.

Double bottom. A chart pattern indicating two subsequent low points, often interpreted as a bullish sign.

DRIPs. Direct reinvestment plans, offered by companies, that allow investors to automatically purchase additional shares with the money they earn from dividend payments.

Ex-dividend date. The date on which the purchaser of a stock does not receive the most recently declared dividend. Any purchase of the stock on that date or after will be ex-dividend. The opening price of the stock will usually be reduced by the value of the dividend. See *record date.*

Financial assets. Investments such as stocks, bonds, and certificates of deposit.

Fiscal year. The 12-month accounting period that a company uses for reporting its business activities. The fiscal year may or may not correspond to the regular calendar year. Many companies maintain fiscal years that are different from calendar years due to the physical nature or business cycle of their industries.

Frictional costs. The charges related to the buying and selling of investments, namely, commissions and taxes.

Full-service brokerage. A brokerage house that offers its customers more than basic trading services, such as research, though they generally charge higher commissions than their discount counterparts.

Fundamental analysis. Researching a stock by looking at the financial health of its underlying company.

Futures. Contracts that enable their holder to buy or sell an underlying investment at a predetermined price. A futures holder must exercise the contract on its expiration date.

Gap. A space on a chart between a closing price and the next trading day's opening price, indicating significant price movement without the occurrence of buying or selling.

Good till cancelled. A stock order that remains open until it's either filled or cancelled.

Goodwill. Goodwill represents the value of a company's brand name, loyal customer base, reputation for high quality products, and other similar intangible assets that provide it with above-average earnings power.

Hedge fund. A largely unregulated private investment fund that can invest any way it chooses.

Hedging. An investment position utilizing offsetting securities positions to minimize the risk of a financial loss.

Income statement. A detailed summary of the income and expenses of a business over a specified period of time, showing the net profit or loss for that period.

Index. A numerical representation of a given sector or market's performance, arrived at by computing the price movements of one or more constituents.

Index fund. A mutual fund that attempts to match the performance of a major market index, such as the S&P 500. An index fund generally holds all of the securities included in a particular stock or bond market index in the same proportion as they are represented in the index.

Inflation. Refers to the rise in the general price level for goods and services over a period of time.

Initial public offering (IPO). A company's first sale of stock to the public, usually underwritten by a single investment banker or a pool of investment bankers and brokerage firms.

Insider. Anyone having access to material corporate information. The term is generally used to indicate corporate officers and boards of directors.

Insider trading. The buying or selling of a stock by someone involved in the underlying company's day-to-day affairs, particularly someone in a managerial position; buying or selling stock on the basis of nonpublic information.

Junk bond. Also known as *high yield bonds*, these are issued by companies that carry a speculative credit rating. A bond that has an S&P credit rating of less than BBB is considered a speculative grade bond.

Laddered portfolio. A fixed-income portfolio constructed of bonds with equally spaced maturities.

LEAPS. Long-term Equity AnticiPation Securities are essentially options that are valid for years rather than months.

Leverage. In investing, being able to control a larger investment than one has paid for upfront.

Leveraged buyout (LBO). A transaction used to take a corporation private, financed to a large degree by debt that is secured, serviced, and repaid through the cash flow and assets of the acquired firm.

Limit order. Tells a broker to buy or sell stock at or better than a specified price.

Liquidity. The ease with which an investment can be bought, sold, or turned into cash.

Margin account. An account that allows an investor to purchase additional stock with money borrowed against stock and cash already in an investment account.

Margin call. When a brokerage house orders an investor on margin to either place additional funds in an investment account or face the possibility of having other investments sold off to pay for mounting losses on margined securities.

Market capitalization. A company's value based on the worth of its outstanding public stock; the number of shares outstanding times the current price of the stock.

Market makers. Professionals who facilitate the buying and selling of stock on the Nasdaq market.

Market order. Tells a broker to buy or sell stock at the best current price available.

Money market. A safe, liquid form of mutual fund commonly used as a short-term place for keeping money. Generally provides higher returns than traditional savings accounts.

Moving average. A statistical tool used by technical analysts to determine the momentum of an investment.

Municipal bonds. Bonds issued by towns, cities, or other local government agencies.

Naked put. Writing a put option when the underlying stock is not owned.

Net asset value (NAV). The market value of stocks, bonds, and net cash divided by outstanding shares.

Net income. Income after all taxes and expenses have been subtracted. Also called *net profit* and *after-tax profit*. Essentially, a company's earnings.

Open-end fund. A mutual fund that issues new shares when investors put in money and redeems shares when investors withdraw money. (See *closed-end fund.*)

Opportunity cost. The difference between two different investment options; for example, the advantages lost when another investment strategy is pursued.

Options. Contracts that allow their holder to either buy or sell stock at a predetermined price.

PEG ratio. A stock's P/E ratio divided by its expected earnings growth rate. See *price-to-earnings ratio.*

Physical assets. Tangible goods.

Portfolio. The collection of investments held by a particular investor or group of investors.

Preferred stock. Class of stock that entitles holders to greater privileges than holders of common stock, including greater voting power and higher priority in the event of liquidation.

Price-to-earnings ratio (P/E ratio). A company's current stock price divided by its underlying earnings.

Price-to-sales ratio. A company's current stock price divided by the underlying company's annual revenue.

Principal. The primary sum of money either invested or borrowed, on which interest is usually paid.

Private placement. A block of stock or bonds that is supplied directly to investors, rather than through the public markets.

Put option. A contract giving the holder the right to sell the underlying security at a specific price during a specified period of time.

Record date. When dividends are declared, a record date is set that marks the day an investor must officially own the stock in order to be entitled to the dividend. Two days prior to the record date, the stock will trade *ex-dividend*.

REITs. Real Estate Investment Trusts; companies that own large properties and distribute most of their earnings to their investors.

Resistance. In technical analysis, an area of resistance on a chart is a price range, above the current price, that would likely spark selling interest.

Road shows. Marketing events that highlight a company's merits to potential investors.

Secondary market. A place where preexisting investments can be bought and sold.

Secondary offering. A follow-on offering of public stock issued by a company.

Securities and Exchange Commission (SEC). A regulatory agency responsible for administering federal securities laws.

Seed capital. Money used to start a business, often supplied by angel investors.

Shorting. Borrowing shares of stock in the hope that they'll fall, so the borrower can replace the shares at a lower price and keep the difference.

Short squeeze. When a large number of people who have sold short attempt to close out their positions, resulting in a vicious cycle of rising prices and additional shorts attempting to cover.

Specialists. Investment professionals who facilitate trading on the New York Stock Exchange floor.

Stock options. Contracts that allow their holder to either purchase or sell a set amount of stock at a fixed price over the course of a certain time period.

Stop order. An order that doesn't go into effect until a specified price is reached.

Strike price. The predetermined price at which an underlying security may be bought or sold by means of an option.

Support. In technical analysis, an area of support on a chart is a price range, below the current price, that would likely spark buying interest.

Syndication. In investment banking, syndication involves placing newly issued stock with investors.

Technical analysis. Using charting or computer analysis programs to isolate price and volume movements that are believed to signal future market and individual stock price movements.

Time premium. The portion of an option's price that represents the amount of time left until the option expires.

TIPS. Treasury Inflation-Protected Securities; bonds with yields that are tied to the current rate of inflation.

Total return. Total return is the full amount an investment earns over a specific period of time, including capital appreciation and yield.

Trailing earnings. A company's earnings over the last four completed quarters, regardless of whether those four quarters comprise a calendar year, a fiscal year, or any other official time period.

Turnover ratio. The turnover ratio is usually associated with a mutual fund manager's trading activity. A fund that has a turnover ratio of 100 percent indicates that the entire value of the portfolio has been traded over, or "turned over."

Venture capitalists. Investors who specialize in funding early stage companies.

Volatility. The amount of price movement of a stock, bond, commodity, or the market during a specific period.

Volume. The number of shares of stock that have been traded during a particular period in time.

Yield. The rate of return, expressed as a percentage, paid on a stock in the form of dividends or on a bond as the rate of interest.

Zero coupon bond. Bonds that have no periodic interest payments. The interest earned on a zero coupon bond is the difference between the bond's purchase price and its maturity value.

Index

[207]

About the Author

Nilus Mattive has written for a number of investment companies. He is currently Senior Editor of Standard & Poor's *The Outlook*, which is the oldest continuously published investment advisory newsletter in the country. He lives in New York City.

FREE OFFER—The Oldest and Wisest Investment Newsletter in the Newest and Easiest Format

The *Outlook* is America's oldest continuously published investment advisory newsletter, and now it's available online! Best of all, because you're reading an S&P book, you're entitled to a free 30-day trial. Outlook Online is perfect for both beginners and expert investors alike. The site contains the latest issue of *The Outlook* as well as a searchable archive of the past year's issues. You'll get everything from Standard & Poor's latest individual investment recommendations and economic forecasts to complete portfolios that can help you build wealth. For more than 80 years, *The Outlook* has been identifying the developments that affect stock performance—and making recommendations on when to buy, sell and hold. With Outlook Online you'll also get:

Features on Sectors, Industries and Technical Analysis—These weekly articles will keep you informed about what sectors are poised to outperform, what industries have been on a roll, a where the market may be headed next.

Supervised Master List of Recommended Issues—Standard & Poor's favorites for long-term capital appreciation and superior long-term total return. These groups of stocks have been helping generations of investors build wealth.

Complete Lists of STARS stocks—The highly regarded *Stock Appreciation Ranking System* offers an easy way to pick stocks that Standard & Poor's believes will do best in the near term—six months to one year. Week after week, STARS ranks 1,200 active stocks so you can track changes at a glance.

Platinum and Neural Fair Value Portfolios—Outlook Online also contains detailed information on two more of Standard & Poor's portfolios, both of which have historically outperformed the market by wide margins.

Global Features—Outlook Online is also helpful to investors looking for news and views from abroad. It contains a number of features on both Europe and Asia, including the best picks from S&P's overseas research departments.

Stock and Fund Reports—You'll even get access to 10 free Standard & Poor's reports every month. Whether you're looking for more information on a company or a mutual fund, these reports will help you make informed decisions.

It's simple to activate your free trial to Outlook Online. Just visit the URL below and follow the directions on the screen. No credit card is required and registration will take only a few minutes. To get the best guidance on Wall Street and specific stock recommendations from the experts in the field, just visit us at:
http://www.spoutlookonline.com/ol_mw1.0.asp?ADID=MAT